Microsoft

Implementing, Managing, and Maintaining a Microsoft® Windows Server™ 2003 Network Infrastructure (70-291)

Lab Manual

Michael D. Hall
and
Tony Smith

PUBLISHED BY
Microsoft Press
A Division of Microsoft Corporation
One Microsoft Way
Redmond, Washington 98052-6399

Printed and bound in the United States of America.

3 4 5 6 7 8 9   QWT   8 7 6

Distributed in Canada by H.B. Fenn and Company Ltd.

A CIP catalogue record for this book is available from the British Library.

Microsoft Press books are available through booksellers and distributors worldwide. For further information about international editions, contact your local Microsoft Corporation office or contact Microsoft Press International directly at fax (425)
936-7329. Visit our Web site at www.microsoft.com/mspress. Send comments to *moac@microsoft.com*.

Program Managers: Hilary Long, Linda Engelman
Project Editor: Julie Miller
Technical Editor: Owen Fowler
Copy Editors: Ginny Bess, Chrstina Palaia (BookMasters, Inc.)

Sub Assy Part No. X10-23970
Body Part No. X10-23975

CONTENTS

LAB 1
IMPLEMENTING DHCP

This lab contains the following exercises and activities:

■ Exercise 1-1: Using APIPA

■ Exercise 1-2: Installing the DHCP Server Service

■ Exercise 1-3: Authorizing the DHCP Server Service in Active Directory

■ Exercise 1-4: Adding, Configuring, and Activating a DHCP Scope

■ Exercise 1-5: Adding DHCP Client Reservations

■ Exercise 1-6: Configuring DHCP Options

■ Exercise 1-7: Configuring a DHCP Relay Agent

■ Exercise 1-8: Starting the DHCP Server Service

■ Lab Review Questions

■ Lab Challenge 1-1: Converting to Dynamic IP Addressing

After completing this lab, you will be able to:

■ Configure APIPA and manual IP addressing.

■ Add and authorize a DHCP Server service.

■ Configure a DHCP scope.

■ Configure DHCP client reservations.

■ Configure DHCP scope options.

■ Configure a DHCP relay agent.

Estimated completion time: 155 minutes (this estimate includes the Before You Begin setup procedures)

BEFORE YOU BEGIN

Estimated completion time: 10 minutes

To complete the exercises in Lab 1, you are required to install a second network adapter in each of the student's computers. Connect the additional network adapters using a crossover cable between each computer. Table 1-1 will be used to configure the student computers during this lab. However, it is not necessary to make configuration changes at this point. After completing Lab 1, remove the second network adapters or disable them in the Microsoft Windows interface before continuing with subsequent labs.

Table 1-1   Student Computer IP Addressing

Computer Name	Contoso, Ltd., Network	Litware, Inc., Network
Computer01	IP address: 10.1.1.1 Subnet mask: 255.255.0.0	IP address: 192.168.0.1 Subnet mask: 255.255.255.0
Computer02	IP address: 10.1.1.2 Subnet mask: 255.255.0.0	IP address: 192.168.0.2 Subnet mask: 255.255.255.0
Computer03	IP address: 10.1.1.3 Subnet mask: 255.255.0.0	IP address: 192.168.0.3 Subnet mask: 255.255.255.0
Computer04	IP address: 10.1.1.4 Subnet mask: 255.255.0.0	IP address: 192.168.0.4 Subnet mask: 255.255.255.0
Computer05	IP address: 10.1.1.5 Subnet mask: 255.255.0.0	IP address: 192.168.0.5 Subnet mask: 255.255.255.0
Computer06	IP address: 10.1.1.6 Subnet mask: 255.255.0.0	IP address: 192.168.0.6 Subnet mask: 255.255.255.0
Computer07	IP address: 10.1.1.7 Subnet mask: 255.255.0.0	IP address: 192.168.0.7 Subnet mask: 255.255.255.0
Computer08	IP address: 10.1.1.8 Subnet mask: 255.255.0.0	IP address: 192.168.0.8 Subnet mask: 255.255.255.0
Computer09	IP address: 10.1.1.9 Subnet mask: 255.255.0.0	IP address: 192.168.0.9 Subnet mask: 255.255.255.0
Computer10	IP address: 10.1.1.10 Subnet mask: 255.255.0.0	IP address: 192.168.0.10 Subnet mask: 255.255.255.0
Computer11	IP address: 10.1.1.11 Subnet mask: 255.255.0.0	IP address: 192.168.0.11 Subnet mask: 255.255.255.0
Computer12	IP address: 10.1.1.12 Subnet mask: 255.255.0.0	IP address: 192.168.0.12 Subnet mask: 255.255.255.0
Computer13	IP address: 10.1.1.13 Subnet mask: 255.255.0.0	IP address: 192.168.0.13 Subnet mask: 255.255.255.0
Computer14	IP address: 10.1.1.14 Subnet mask: 255.255.0.0	IP address: 192.168.0.14 Subnet mask: 255.255.255.0
Computer15	IP address: 10.1.1.15 Subnet mask: 255.255.0.0	IP address: 192.168.0.15 Subnet mask: 255.255.255.0
Computer16	IP address: 10.1.1.16 Subnet mask: 255.255.0.0	IP address: 192.168.0.16 Subnet mask: 255.255.255.0
Computer17	IP address: 10.1.1.17 Subnet mask: 255.255.0.0	IP address: 192.168.0.17 Subnet mask: 255.255.255.0
Computer18	IP address: 10.1.1.18 Subnet mask: 255.255.0.0	IP address: 192.168.0.18 Subnet mask: 255.255.255.0
Computer19	IP address: 10.1.1.19 Subnet mask: 255.255.0.0	IP address: 192.168.0.19 Subnet mask: 255.255.255.0
Computer20	IP address: 10.1.1.20 Subnet mask: 255.255.0.0	IP address: 192.168.0.20 Subnet mask: 255.255.255.0
Computer21	IP address: 10.1.1.21 Subnet mask: 255.255.0.0	IP address: 192.168.0.21 Subnet mask: 255.255.255.0
Computer22	IP address: 10.1.1.22 Subnet mask: 255.255.0.0	IP address: 192.168.0.22 Subnet mask: 255.255.255.0
Computer23	IP address: 10.1.1.23 Subnet mask: 255.255.0.0	IP address: 192.168.0.23 Subnet mask: 255.255.255.0

(continued)

Table 1-1   Student Computer IP Addressing

Computer Name	Contoso, Ltd., Network	Litware, Inc., Network
Computer24	IP address: 10.1.1.24 Subnet mask: 255.255.0.0	IP address: 192.168.0.24 Subnet mask: 255.255.255.0
Computer25	IP address: 10.1.1.25 Subnet mask: 255.255.0.0	IP address: 192.168.0.25 Subnet mask: 255.255.255.0
Computer26	IP address: 10.1.1.26 Subnet mask: 255.255.0.0	IP address: 192.168.0.26 Subnet mask: 255.255.255.0
Computer27	IP address: 10.1.1.27 Subnet mask: 255.255.0.0	IP address: 192.168.0.27 Subnet mask: 255.255.255.0
Computer28	IP address: 10.1.1.28 Subnet mask: 255.255.0.0	IP address: 192.168.0.28 Subnet mask: 255.255.255.0
Computer29	IP address: 10.1.1.29 Subnet mask: 255.255.0.0	IP address: 192.168.0.29 Subnet mask: 255.255.255.0
Computer30	IP address: 10.1.1.30 Subnet mask: 255.255.0.0	IP address: 192.168.0.30 Subnet mask: 255.255.255.0

SCENARIO

You are a network administrator for Litware, Inc. Recently, Contoso, Ltd., acquired Litware, Inc. As a result, Litware, Inc., is expanding its network. In the past, Litware, Inc., utilized Automatic Private IP Addressing (APIPA). Because of the increase in the number of clients (which motivated Contoso to acquire Litware, Inc.) and the fact that network administrators installed a router to allow users Internet access, you have been asked to plan and install a dynamic addressing system using Dynamic Host Configuration Protocol (DHCP). You and a partner must work together to install the DHCP Server service and configure it to assign the necessary configuration parameters.

EXERCISE 1-1: USING APIPA

Estimated completion time: 15 minutes

In this exercise, you will configure a static IP address on your Litware Inc Network adapter. Next, you will view and verify the Transmission Control Protocol/Internet Protocol (TCP/IP) configuration information assigned to the adapters.

Viewing Manual IP Addressing Information

> **IMPORTANT**   Complete this task from both student computers. This will allow you to view the manual IP addressing information configured on the server computer.

1. Start your computer running Microsoft Windows Server 2003, and log on as **administrator@*domain*.contoso.com** (where *domain* is the name of your domain).

2. Click Start, select Run, type **cmd**, and then press Enter.

3. At the command prompt type **ipconfig /all**, and then press Enter.

4. Record the following Contoso, Ltd. Network adapter IP information:

   a. IP address: _169,254,227, 171_

   b. Subnet mask: _255,255, 0, 0_

   c. Default gateway: _____

   d. DNS server: _10,1,1,200_

QUESTION Where did the computer receive its IP address for the Contoso, Ltd. Network adapter?

Viewing APIPA Addressing Information

IMPORTANT Complete this task from both student computers. Also verify that the crossover cable is connected between the two student computers.

1. Using the same steps, record the Litware Inc Network adapter IP addressing information in the following list:

   a. IP address: _10,1,1,1_

   b. Subnet mask: _255, 255, 0,0_

   c. Default gateway: _____

   d. DNS server: _10,1, 1,200_

QUESTION Where did the Litware Inc Network adapter receive its IP addressing information? Why did it receive it from that source?

2. To close the command prompt window, type **exit**.

Entering Static IP Addressing Information into the Litware, Inc. Network Adapter

IMPORTANT Complete this task from both student computers. This will allow you to configure a static IP address on the Litware, Inc. Network adapter. Use the IP addressing information in Table 1-1 to obtain the correct IP address for the Litware, Inc. Network adapter.

1. Right-click the Litware Inc Network connection.

2. Select Properties.

3. Highlight Internet Protocol (TCP/IP) in the list of components, and then click Properties.

4. Select the Use The Following IP Address option.

5. Enter the IP addressing information from Table 1-1.

6. Click OK to accept the changes to the TCP/IP addressing properties.

7. Click Close to accept the network connection changes.

EXERCISE 1-2: INSTALLING THE DHCP SERVER SERVICE

Estimated completion time: 10 minutes

To prepare for dynamic address assignment, you will now install the DHCP Server service.

> **IMPORTANT** *Complete this task from both student computers. This will allow you to configure your server as a DHCP server.*

1. Start your computer running Windows Server 2003, and log on as **student*xx*@*domain*.contoso.com** (where student*xx* is the name of your student User Name and *domain* is the name of your domain).

2. Click Start, click Control Panel, and then double-click Administrative Tools. Right-click Manage Your Server, and select Run As to open the Run As dialog box.

3. In the Run As dialog box, select The Following User Option and enter the following credentials to open the Manage Your Server page:

    a. In the User box, type **administrator@*domain*.contoso.com**.

    b. In the Password box, type **MSPress@LS#1**.

4. On the Manage Your Server page, click Add Or Remove A Role, and then click Next.

5. In the Configure Your Server Wizard, select DHCP Server, and then click Next.

6. On the Summary Of Selections page, click Next.

7. In the New Scope Wizard, click Cancel to discontinue creating a scope at this time.

8. In the Configure Your Server Wizard, click Finish.

EXERCISE 1-3: AUTHORIZING THE DHCP SERVER SERVICE IN ACTIVE DIRECTORY

Estimated completion time: 10 minutes

Now that the DHCP Server service is installed, you must authorize it in Active Directory directory service.

Authorizing the DHCP Server Service

> **IMPORTANT** *Complete this task from both student computers. This will allow you to authorize your DHCP server in Active Directory.*

1. Start your computer running Windows Server 2003, and log on as **student*xx*@*domain*.contoso.com** (where student*xx* is the name of your student User Name and *domain* is the name of your domain).

2. Click the Start button and select Control Panel. In the Control Panel, double-click Administrative Tools.

3. Right-click DHCP and select Run As to open the Run As dialog box.

4. In the Run As dialog box, select The Following User option and enter the following credentials in the dialog box fields to open the DHCP console:

   a. In the User Name box, type **eadmin@contoso.com**.

   b. For the Password option, type **MSPress@LS#1**.

5. Click OK to open the DHCP console.

6. In the console tree, select your server name, Computer*xx.domain*.contoso.com.

7. Right-click your server name.

8. On the pop-up menu, click Authorize.

9. To verify that the DHCP server is authorized, in the console tree, press F5.

10. The console tree should now display a green arrow.

QUESTION *Why do we have to authorize the DHCP server?*

EXERCISE 1-4: ADDING, CONFIGURING, AND ACTIVATING A DHCP SCOPE

Estimated completion time: 15 minutes

The DHCP Server service is now installed and the server is authorized in Active Directory. The next step is to configure and activate a DHCP scope. When the scope has been created and activated, the partner with the higher computer number will change the TCP/IP properties setting and obtain an address from the DHCP server.

Adding and Configuring a DHCP Scope

IMPORTANT *Complete this task from both student computers. This will allow you to add a DHCP scope to your partner's computer.*

1. Start your computer running Windows Server 2003, and log on as **student*xx*@*domain*.contoso.com** (where student*xx* is the name of your student User Name and *domain* is the name of your domain).

2. Click the Start button and select Control Panel. In the Control Panel, double-click Administrative Tools.

3. Right-click DHCP and select Run As to open the Run As dialog box.

4. In the Run As dialog box, select The Following User option and enter the following credentials in the dialog box fields to open the DHCP console:

   a. In the User box, type **administrator@*domain*.contoso.com**.

   b. In the Password box, type **MSPress@LS#1**.

5. Click OK to open the DHCP console.

6. Select the applicable DHCP server from the console tree.

7. On the Action menu, select New Scope to create a new DHCP scope.

8. In the New Scope Wizard, click Next.

9. On the Scope Name page, configure the following:

   a. For Name, enter **partner's computer scope**.

   b. For Description, enter **scope for partner's computer**.

10. On the IP Address Range page, configure the following:

    a. For the Start IP Address, enter your partner's Litware Inc Network connection IP address.

    b. For the End IP Address, enter your partner's Litware Inc Network connection IP address.

    c. For the Subnet Mask, enter **24 bit** or **255.255.255.0**.

11. On the Add Exclusions page, click Next.

12. On the Lease Duration page, select 1 hour, and then click Next.

13. On the Configure DHCP Options page, select No, I Will Configure These Options Later. Click Next.

14. On the Completing The New Scope Wizard page, click Finish.

Activating a DHCP Scope

IMPORTANT   Complete this task from both student computers. This will allow you to activate a DHCP scope.

1. Start your computer running Windows Server 2003, and log on as **student*xx*@*domain*.contoso.com** (where student*xx* is the name of your student User Name and *domain* is the name of your domain).

2. Click the Start button and select Control Panel. In the Control Panel, double-click Administrative Tools.

3. Right-click DHCP and select Run As to open the Run As dialog box.

4. In the Run As dialog box, select The Following User option and enter the following credentials in the dialog box fields to open the DHCP console:

   a. In the User box, type **administrator@*domain*.contoso.com**.

   b. In the Password box, type **MSPress@LS#1**.

5. Click OK to open the DHCP console.

6. Select the name of your server in the console tree.

7. Select the scope named **Partner's Computer Scope**.

8. On the Action menu, select Activate.

9. Close the DHCP MMC console.

QUESTION Why do you have to activate a DHCP scope?

Stopping the DHCP Server Service

IMPORTANT Complete this task from the computer with the higher number. This will allow you to obtain an IP address leased from a DHCP server.

1. Start your computer running Windows Server 2003, and log on as **student*xx*@*domain*.contoso.com** (where student*xx* is the name of your student User Name and *domain* is the name of your domain).

2. Click the Start button and select Control Panel. In the Control Panel, double-click Administrative Tools.

3. Right-click DHCP and select Run As to open the Run As dialog box.

4. In the Run As dialog box, select The Following User option and enter the following credentials in the dialog box fields to open the DHCP console:

   a. In the User box, type **administrator@*domain*.contoso.com**.

   b. In the Password box, type **MSPress@LS#1**.

5. Click OK to open the DHCP console.

6. In the DHCP console window, first select and then right-click DHCP Server.

7. In the pop-up menu, select All Tasks, and then select Stop.

8. Close all windows.

Obtaining a DHCP Lease IP Address

IMPORTANT Complete this task from the computer with the higher number. This will allow you to obtain an IP address leased from a DHCP server.

1. Start your computer running Windows Server 2003, and log on as **administrator@*domain*.contoso.com** (where *domain* is the name of your domain).

2. Click Start, and then select Network Connections.

3. Right-click the Litware Inc Network connection icon.

4. Select Properties.

5. Select Internet Protocol (TCP/IP) in the list of components, and then click Properties. Select Obtain An IP Address Automatically.

6. Click OK to accept the changes to the TCP/IP addressing properties.

7. Click Close to accept the network connection changes.

8. Click Start, and then select Run.

9. Type **cmd**, and then press Enter.

10. In the command prompt window, type **ipconfig /renew**.

11. In the command prompt window, type **ipconfig /all**.

12. Verify that the IP address listed for the Litware Inc Network connection is the IP address configured on your partner's DHCP server. Also, verify that its DHCP server has the IP address of your partner's computer.

Verifying the DHCP Leased IP Address

> **IMPORTANT**   Complete this task from the computer with the lower number. This will allow you to view the IP address leased from a DHCP server.

1. Start your computer running Windows Server 2003, and log on as **studentxx@*domain*.contoso.com** (where studentxx is the name of your student User Name and *domain* is the name of your domain).

2. Click the Start button and select Control Panel. In the Control Panel, double-click Administrative Tools.

3. Right-click DHCP and select Run As to open the Run As dialog box.

4. In the Run As dialog box, select The Following User option and enter the following credentials in the dialog box fields to open the DHCP console:

   a. In the User Name box, type **administrator@*domain*.contoso.com**.

   b. In the Password box, type **MSPress@LS#1**.

5. Click OK to open the DHCP console.

6. Select the name of your server in the console tree.

7. Select the scope named **Partner's Computer Scope**.

8. Select the Address Leases node.

9. Verify that Computer*xx.domain*.contoso.com is listed under the Name column in the Address Leases pane.

EXERCISE 1-5: ADDING DHCP CLIENT RESERVATIONS

Estimated completion time: 10 minutes

In certain situations, such as reserving an IP address for a print server, you need a DHCP client to receive the same IP address each time. This can be done using client reservations through DHCP. In this exercise, you will configure client reservations on each of your DHCP servers.

Adding a DHCP Client Reservation

IMPORTANT   *Complete this task from the student computer with the lower number. This will allow you to configure a client reservation for a DHCP client.*

1. Start your computer running Windows Server 2003, and log on as **studentxx@*domain*.contoso.com** (where studentxx is the name of your student User Name and *domain* is the name of your domain).

2. Click the Start button and select Control Panel. In the Control Panel, double-click Administrative Tools.

3. Right-click DHCP and select Run As to open the Run As dialog box.

4. In the Run As dialog box, select The Following User Option and enter the following credentials in the dialog box fields to open the DHCP console:

    a. In the User Name box, type **administrator@*domain*.contoso.com.**

    b. In the Password box, type **MSPress@LS#1**.

5. Click OK to open the DHCP console.

6. Select the applicable DHCP server in the console tree.

7. Expand the applicable DHCP server, then expand the Partner's Computer Scope node.

8. In the console tree, click Reservations. On the Action menu, select New Reservation.

9. In the Reservation Name box, type the name of your partner's computer.

10. In the IP Address box, type the IP address of the Litware network connection.

11. In the MAC Address box, type the MAC address of your partner's network connection.

12. In the Description box, type **client reservation**.

13. In the Supported Types box, select DHCP Only.

14. Click Add to add the client reservation.

15. Click Close.

Obtaining a DHCP Client Reservation IP Address

IMPORTANT   *Complete this task from the student computer with the higher number. This will allow you to obtain an IP address that has been reserved on a DHCP server.*

1. Start your computer running Windows Server 2003, and log on as **studentxx@*domain*.contoso.com** (where studentxx is the name of your student User Name and *domain* is the name of your domain).

2. From the Start menu, point to All Programs, point to Accessories, right-click Command Prompt, and then select Run As to open the Run As dialog box.

3. In the Run As dialog box, select The Following User option and enter the following credentials in the dialog box fields to open the command prompt window:

   a. In the User Name box, type **administrator@*domain*.contoso.com.**

   b. In the Password box, type **MSPress@LS#1**.

4. Click OK to open the command prompt window.

5. In the command prompt window, type **ipconfig /renew**.

6. In the command prompt window, type **ipconfig /all**.

7. Verify that the IP address listed for the Litware Inc Network connection is the IP address configured on your partner's DHCP server.

Verifying a DHCP Client Reservation IP Address

IMPORTANT   *Complete this task from the student computer with the lower number. This will allow you to verify that a DHCP server has reserved an IP address for the DHCP client computer.*

1. Start your computer running Windows Server 2003, and log on as **student*xx*@*domain*.contoso.com** (where student*xx* is the name of your student User Name and *domain* is the name of your domain).

2. Click the Start button and select Control Panel. In the Control Panel, double-click Administrative Tools.

3. Right-click DHCP and select Run As to open the Run As dialog box.

4. In the Run As dialog box, select The Following User option and enter the following credentials in the dialog box fields to open the DHCP console:

   a. In the User Name box, type **administrator@*domain*.contoso.com.**

   b. In the Password box, type **MSPress@LS#1**.

5. Click OK to open the DHCP console.

6. In the DHCP console tree, select the applicable DHCP server, then expand the Partner's Computer Scope node.

7. In the console tree, click Address Leases.

8. Verify that the reservation displays as active.

9. In the DHCP console, under Address Leases, delete the client reservation.

EXERCISE 1-6: CONFIGURING DHCP OPTIONS

Estimated completion time: 10 minutes

DHCP scope options allow an administrator to dynamically assign additional information, such as the address of a DNS server or default gateway. In this exercise, you will configure your DHCP server to assign the address of the default gateway.

Configuring DHCP Scope Options

IMPORTANT   *Complete this task from the student computer with the lower number. This will allow you to configure DHCP scope-level options for DHCP clients.*

1. Start your computer running Windows Server 2003, and log on as **studentxx@domain.contoso.com** (where studentxx is the name of your student User Name and *domain* is the name of your domain).

2. Click the Start button and select Control Panel. In the Control Panel, double-click Administrative Tools.

3. Right-click DHCP and select Run As to open the Run As dialog box.

4. In the Run As dialog box, select The Following User option and enter the following credentials in the dialog box fields to open the DHCP console:

    a. In the User Name box, type **administrator@domain.contoso.com.**

    b. In the Password box, type **MSPress@LS#1**.

5. Click OK to open the DHCP console.

6. Select the applicable DHCP server in the DHCP console tree.

7. In the console tree, expand the Partner's Computer Scope node.

8. Select and then right-click Scope Options, then select Configure Options. In the list of Scope Options, select 003 Router.

9. In the Data Entry IP Address box, type the IP address of your partner's Litware Inc Network connection, and then click Add.

10. Click OK.

QUESTION   *What are other DHCP options that are used on a network?*

Obtaining a DHCP Scope Option

IMPORTANT   *Complete this task from the student computer with the higher number. This will allow you to obtain DHCP scope-level options from a DHCP server.*

1. Start your computer running Windows Server 2003, and log on as **studentxx@domain.contoso.com** (where studentxx is the name of your student User Name and *domain* is the name of your domain).

2. From the Start menu, point to All Programs, point to Accessories, right-click Command Prompt, and then select Run As to open the Run As dialog box.

3. In the Run As dialog box, select The Following User option and enter the following credentials in the dialog box fields to open the command prompt window:

   a. In the User Name box, type **administrator@*domain*.contoso.com.**

   b. In the Password box, type **MSPress@LS#1**.

4. Click OK to open the command prompt window.

5. In the command prompt window, type **ipconfig /renew**.

6. In the command prompt window, type **ipconfig /all**.

7. Verify that the IP address listed for the gateway is the IP address of your partner's network connection.

EXERCISE 1-7: CONFIGURING A DHCP RELAY AGENT

Estimated completion time: 20 minutes

In a network that has client computers separated from the DHCP server by a router that is not configured to forward DHCP broadcasts, you must configure a DHCP relay agent. In this exercise, you first install Routing And Remote Access on your server. You then configure a DHCP relay agent and have your partner's computer receive an IP address.

Add Routing And Remote Access

IMPORTANT   *Only complete the following steps on the lower-numbered student computer. This will allow you to configure your server to act as a local area network (LAN) router.*

1. Start your computer running Windows Server 2003, and log on as **student*xx*@*domain*.contoso.com** (where student*xx* is the name of your student User Name and *domain* is the name of your domain).

2. Click the Start button and select Control Panel. In the Control Panel, double-click Administrative Tools.

3. Right-click Routing And Remote Access and select Run As to open the Run As dialog box.

4. In the Run As dialog box, select The Following User option and enter the following credentials in the dialog box fields to open the Routing And Remote Access console:

   a. In the User Name box, type **administrator@*domain*.contoso.com.**

   b. In the Password box, type **MSPress@LS#1**.

5. Click OK to open the Routing And Remote Access console.

6. In the Routing And Remote Access console, select the computer name, then select the Action menu, and select Configure And Enable Routing And Remote Access.

7. In the Routing And Remote Access Server Setup Wizard, click Next.

8. On the Configuration page, click Custom Configuration, and then click Next.

9. On the Custom Configuration page, click LAN Routing, and then click Next.

10. On the Completing The Routing And Remote Access Server Setup Wizard page, click Finish.

11. When it prompts you to start the service, click Yes.

Adding the Routing Information Protocol (RIP)

IMPORTANT Only complete the following steps on the lower-numbered student computer. This will allow you to configure your server with RIP to allow it to route or forward packets.

1. Start your computer running Windows Server 2003, and log on as **studentxx@_domain_.contoso.com** (where studentxx is the name of your student User Name and *domain* is the name of your domain).

2. Click the Start button and select Control Panel. In the Control Panel, double-click Administrative Tools.

3. Right-click Routing And Remote Access and select Run As to open the Run As dialog box.

4. In the Run As dialog box, select The Following User option and enter the following credentials in the dialog box fields to open the Routing and Remote Access console:

   a. In the User Name box, type **administrator@_domain_.contoso.com.**

   b. In the Password box, type **MSPress@LS#1**.

5. Click OK to open the Routing And Remote Access console.

6. In the Routing And Remote Access console, expand Computer.xx, then select IP Routing.

7. Under IP Routing, right-click General, and then select New Routing Protocol.

8. On the New Routing Protocol page, click RIP Version 2 For Internet Protocol, and then click OK.

   QUESTION What are two methods to enable packets to be delivered to the other subnet?

9. In the Routing And Remote Access console, right-click RIP, and then select New Interface.

10. On the New Interface For RIP Version 2 For Internet Protocol dialog box, under Interfaces, select Contoso Corp Network, and then click OK.

11. On the RIP Properties-Contoso Corp Network Properties page, click OK.

12. In the Routing And Remote Access console, right-click RIP, and then select New Interface.

13. On the New Interface For RIP Version 2 For Internet Protocol dialog box, under Interfaces, select Litware Corp Network, and then click OK.

14. On the RIP Properties-Litware Corp Network Properties page, click OK.

Adding a DHCP Relay Agent

IMPORTANT *Complete the following steps only on the lower-numbered student computer. This will allow you to configure your server as a DHCP relay agent.*

1. Start your computer running Windows Server 2003, and log on as **student*xx*@*domain*.contoso.com** (where student*xx* is the name of your student User Name and *domain* is the name of your domain).

2. Click the Start button and select Control Panel. In the Control Panel, double-click Administrative Tools.

3. Right-click Routing And Remote Access and select Run As to open the Run As dialog box.

4. In the Run As dialog box, select The Following User option and enter the following credentials in the dialog box fields to open the Routing And Remote Access console:

    a. In the User Name box, type **administrator@*domain*.contoso.com.**

    b. In the Password box, type **MSPress@LS#1**.

5. Click OK to open the Routing And Remote Access console.

6. In the Routing And Remote Access console, select IP Routing.

7. Under IP Routing, right-click General, and then select New Routing Protocol.

8. On the New Routing Protocol page, click DHCP Relay Agent, and then click OK.

9. To enable the DHCP relay agent on a router interface, in the console tree, select DHCP Relay Agent.

10. Right-click DHCP Relay Agent, and then select New Interface.

11. Select the Litware Inc Network connection, and then click OK.

12. Verify that the Relay DHCP Packets option is selected.

13. Click OK.

14. To configure the DHCP relay agent interface with the IP address of the DHCP server, open the Routing And Remote Access console.

15. Right-click DHCP Relay Agent, and then select Properties.

16. In the General tab, in the Server Address box, type the IP address of the instructor's computer (**10.1.1.200**), and then click Add.

17. Click OK.

    QUESTION *What would happen if the IP address was not entered in the DHCP relay agent configuration?*

Stopping the DHCP Server Service

IMPORTANT   Complete this task from the computer with the lower number. This will allow you to obtain an IP address leased from a DHCP server.

1. Start your computer running Windows Server 2003, and log on as **studentxx@domain.contoso.com** (where studentxx is the name of your student User Name and *domain* is the name of your domain).

2. Click the Start button and select Control Panel. In the Control Panel, double-click Administrative Tools.

3. Right-click DHCP and select Run As to open the Run As dialog box.

4. In the Run As dialog box, select The Following User option and enter the following credentials in the dialog box fields to open the DHCP console:

   a. In the User Name box, type **administrator@domain.contoso.com.**

   b. In the Password box, type **MSPress@LS#1**.

5. Click OK to open the DHCP console.

6. In the left-hand DHCP console window, first select and then right-click DHCP Server.

7. In the pop-up menu, select All Tasks, and then select Stop.

8. Close all windows.

QUESTION   Why do you have to stop the DHCP Server service on the DHCP relay agent?

Verifying the DHCP Relay Agent

IMPORTANT   Complete the following steps on only the higher-numbered student computer. This will allow you to configure your server as a DHCP relay agent.

1. Start your computer running Windows Server 2003, and log on as **studentxx@domain.contoso.com** (where studentxx is the name of your student User Name and *domain* is the name of your domain).

2. From the Start menu, point to All Programs, point to Accessories, right-click Command Prompt, and then select Run As to open the Run As dialog box.

3. In the Run As dialog box, select The Following User option and enter the following credentials in the dialog box fields to open the command prompt window:

   a. In the User Name box, type **administrator@domain.contoso.com.**

   b. In the Password box, type **MSPress@LS#1**.

4. Click OK to open the command prompt window.

5. In the command prompt window, type **ipconfig /renew**.

6. In the command prompt window, type **ipconfig /all**.

7. Verify that the IP address assigned was from the instructor's computer.

Removing the Routing And Remote Access Service

IMPORTANT   Only complete the following steps on the student computer with the lower number. This will allow you to remove Routing And Remote Access from your server.

1. Start your computer running Windows Server 2003, and log on as **student*xx*@*domain*.contoso.com** (where student*xx* is the name of your student User Name and *domain* is the name of your domain).

2. Click the Start button and select Control Panel. In the Control Panel, double-click Administrative Tools.

3. Right-click Routing And Remote Access and select Run As to open the Run As dialog box.

4. In the Run As dialog box, select The Following User option and enter the following credentials in the dialog box fields to open the Routing And Remote Access console:

   a. In the User Name box, type **administrator@*domain*.contoso.com.**

   b. In the Password box type **MSPress@LS#1**.

5. Click OK to open the Routing And Remote Access console.

6. Right-click the computer.*xx* server name in the Routing And Remote Access console, and then select Disable Routing And Remote Access.

7. In the Routing And Remote Access dialog box, click Yes to remove Routing And Remote Access.

NOTE   DHCP client and DHCP relay agent roles can be reversed if time permits.

EXERCISE 1-8: STARTING THE DHCP SERVER SERVICE

Estimated completion time: 5 minutes

You will now start the DHCP Server service on your student computers.

IMPORTANT   This exercise is necessary for the successful completion of future labs.

Entering Static IP Addressing Information in the Litware, Inc. Network Adapter

IMPORTANT   Complete this task from the computer with the higher number. This will allow you to configure a static IP address on the Litware, Inc. Network adapter. Use the IP addressing information in Table 1-1 for the correct IP address for the Litware, Inc. Network adapter.

1. Start your computer running Windows Server 2003, and log on as **administrator@*domain*.contoso.com** (where *domain* is the name of your domain).

2. Click Start, and then select Network Connections.

3. Right-click the Litware Inc Network connection, and then select Properties.

4. Highlight Internet Protocol (TCP/IP) in the list of components, and then click Properties.

5. Select the Use The Following IP Address option.

6. Enter the IP addressing information from Table 1-1.

7. Click OK to accept the changes to the TCP/IP addressing properties.

8. Click OK to accept the network connection changes.

Starting the DHCP Server Service

IMPORTANT *Complete the following steps on both student computers. This will allow you to start the DHCP service.*

1. Start your computer running Windows Server 2003, and log on as **student*xx*@*domain*.contoso.com** (where student*xx* is the name of your student User Name and *domain* is the name of your domain).

2. Click the Start button and select Control Panel. In the Control Panel, double-click Administrative Tools.

3. Right-click DHCP and select Run As to open the Run As dialog box.

4. In the Run As dialog box, select The Following User option and enter the following credentials in the dialog box fields to open the DHCP console:

   a. In the User Name box, type **administrator@*domain*.contoso.com.**

   b. In the Password box, type **MSPress@LS#1**.

5. Click OK to open the DHCP console.

6. First select and then right-click DHCP, and then select Add Server.

7. In the Add Server dialog box, in the This Server box, enter the IP address of your Litware Inc. network adapter, and then click OK.

8. Select and then right-click your computer name in the DHCP console tree, point to All Tasks, and then select Start.

9. Close all windows.

LAB REVIEW QUESTIONS

Estimated completion time: 20 minutes

1. Name three methods that can be used to assign IP addresses on a TCP/IP-based network.

2. You have installed the DHCP Server service on a computer running Windows Server 2003. You configure the scope option and activate the scope; however, clients still are receiving a 169.254.*x*.*x* IP address. What should you do?

3. You have configured a DHCP scope with an address range of 192.168.0.1 through 192.168.0.254. You have several servers and printers that use the IP address range of 192.168.0.1 through 192.168.0.20. With the least

amount of administrative effort, how can you prevent duplicate IP addressing?

4. You currently are using a DHCP server on your network. It assigns a default gateway scope option to clients. You use a router with a different IP address to replace a router on your network. The new router allows clients to connect to the Internet; however, clients cannot connect to the Internet using the new router. What should you do?

5. You have installed and configured a DHCP server on your network. You also have a Web server on the same network. The Web server requires the same IP address as the DHCP server. What should you do?

6. You must configure a DHCP relay agent for clients on an IP-based subnet. You install Routing and Remote Access, but what else must you do to enable the DHCP relay agent to function properly?

LAB CHALLENGE 1-1: CONVERTING TO DYNAMIC ADDRESSING

Estimated completion time: 30 minutes

Because of your excellent work planning and installing the dynamic addressing system for Litware, Inc., you have been made the network administrator for Litware's newly acquired subsidiary Trey Research. You have been asked to convert Trey Research's network from static addressing to dynamic addressing using DHCP. Trey Research uses the Class C address space 192.168.1.0. One hundred client computers must obtain addressing information from DHCP. One router and five servers are statically configured with the first 10 addresses in your range. Because the company has adequate address space, you should increase the lease period to 20 days. Each DHCP client should receive the address of the default gateway, which is 192.168.1.1.

Work with a partner to set up this scenario. Have the partner's computer that has the lower number in its name act as the DHCP server, and have the other computer act as a DHCP client. Verify that the client receives the correct configuration by issuing the Ipconfig /all command at the command prompt.

If time permits, reverse the student roles and complete this lab challenge again.

LAB 2
MANAGING AND MONITORING DHCP

This lab contains the following exercises and activities:

- Exercise 2-1: Backing Up and Restoring a DHCP Database

- Exercise 2-2: Compacting the DHCP Database

- Exercise 2-3: The DHCP Audit Log

- Exercise 2-4: Monitoring DHCP Performance

- Exercise 2-5: Resolving Misconfigured Servers and Clients

- Exercise 2-6: Removing Dependencies Between Labs

- Lab Review Questions

- Lab Challenge 2-1: Creating a Backup Strategy for Contoso

- Lab Challenge 2-2: Configuring Dynamic Updates

After completing this lab, you will be able to:

- Manage a Dynamic Host Configuration Protocol (DHCP) server database.

- Monitor a DHCP database.

- Resolve misconfigured DHCP servers and clients.

Estimated completion time: 135 minutes (This estimate includes the Before You Begin setup procedures.)

BEFORE YOU BEGIN

> **IMPORTANT**   If you have not completed the exercises in Lab 1, "Implementing DHCP," you must complete the following prerequisite procedures.

Estimated completion time: 10 minutes

To complete the exercises in Lab 2, you are required to install a second network adapter in each of the student computers. Connect the additional network adapters using crossover cables between them. Use Table 2-1 to configure the student computers during this lab; however, it is not necessary to make configuration changes at this point. After completing Lab 2, remove the second network adapters or disable them in the Microsoft Windows interface before continuing with subsequent labs.

Table 2-1   Student Computer IP Addressing

Computer Name	Contoso, Ltd., Network	Litware, Inc., Network
Computer01	IP address: 10.1.1.1 Subnet mask: 255.255.0.0	IP address: 192.168.0.1 Subnet mask: 255.255.255.0
Computer02	IP address: 10.1.1.2 Subnet mask: 255.255.0.0	IP address: 192.168.0.2 Subnet mask: 255.255.255.0
Computer03	IP address: 10.1.1.3 Subnet mask: 255.255.0.0	IP address: 192.168.0.3 Subnet mask: 255.255.255.0
Computer04	IP address: 10.1.1.4 Subnet mask: 255.255.0.0	IP address: 192.168.0.4 Subnet mask: 255.255.255.0
Computer05	IP address: 10.1.1.5 Subnet mask: 255.255.0.0	IP address: 192.168.0.5 Subnet mask: 255.255.255.0
Computer06	IP address: 10.1.1.6 Subnet mask: 255.255.0.0	IP address: 192.168.0.6 Subnet mask: 255.255.255.0
Computer07	IP address: 10.1.1.7 Subnet mask: 255.255.0.0	IP address: 192.168.0.7 Subnet mask: 255.255.255.0
Computer08	IP address: 10.1.1.8 Subnet mask: 255.255.0.0	IP address: 192.168.0.8 Subnet mask: 255.255.255.0
Computer09	IP address: 10.1.1.9 Subnet mask: 255.255.0.0	IP address: 192.168.0.9 Subnet mask: 255.255.255.0
Computer10	IP address: 10.1.1.10 Subnet mask: 255.255.0.0	IP address: 192.168.0.10 Subnet mask: 255.255.255.0
Computer11	IP address: 10.1.1.11 Subnet mask: 255.255.0.0	IP address: 192.168.0.11 Subnet mask: 255.255.255.0
Computer12	IP address: 10.1.1.12 Subnet mask: 255.255.0.0	IP address: 192.168.0.12 Subnet mask: 255.255.255.0
Computer13	IP address: 10.1.1.13 Subnet mask: 255.255.0.0	IP address: 192.168.0.13 Subnet mask: 255.255.255.0
Computer14	IP address: 10.1.1.14 Subnet mask: 255.255.0.0	IP address: 192.168.0.14 Subnet mask: 255.255.255.0
Computer15	IP address: 10.1.1.15 Subnet mask: 255.255.0.0	IP address: 192.168.0.15 Subnet mask: 255.255.255.0
Computer16	IP address: 10.1.1.16 Subnet mask: 255.255.0.0	IP address: 192.168.0.16 Subnet mask: 255.255.255.0
Computer17	IP address: 10.1.1.17 Subnet mask: 255.255.0.0	IP address: 192.168.0.17 Subnet mask: 255.255.255.0
Computer18	IP address: 10.1.1.18 Subnet mask: 255.255.0.0	IP address: 192.168.0.18 Subnet mask: 255.255.255.0
Computer19	IP address: 10.1.1.19 Subnet mask: 255.255.0.0	IP address: 192.168.0.19 Subnet mask: 255.255.255.0
Computer20	IP address: 10.1.1.20 Subnet mask: 255.255.0.0	IP address: 192.168.0.20 Subnet mask: 255.255.255.0
Computer21	IP address: 10.1.1.21 Subnet mask: 255.255.0.0	IP address: 192.168.0.21 Subnet mask: 255.255.255.0
Computer22	IP address: 10.1.1.22 Subnet mask: 255.255.0.0	IP address: 192.168.0.22 Subnet mask: 255.255.255.0
Computer23	IP address: 10.1.1.23 Subnet mask: 255.255.0.0	IP address: 192.168.0.23 Subnet mask: 255.255.255.0

Table 2-1   Student Computer IP Addressing

Computer Name	Contoso, Ltd., Network	Litware, Inc., Network
Computer24	IP address: 10.1.1.24 Subnet mask: 255.255.0.0	IP address: 192.168.0.24 Subnet mask: 255.255.255.0
Computer25	IP address: 10.1.1.25 Subnet mask: 255.255.0.0	IP address: 192.168.0.25 Subnet mask: 255.255.255.0
Computer26	IP address: 10.1.1.26 Subnet mask: 255.255.0.0	IP address: 192.168.0.26 Subnet mask: 255.255.255.0
Computer27	IP address: 10.1.1.27 Subnet mask: 255.255.0.0	IP address: 192.168.0.27 Subnet mask: 255.255.255.0
Computer28	IP address: 10.1.1.28 Subnet mask: 255.255.0.0	IP address: 192.168.0.28 Subnet mask: 255.255.255.0
Computer29	IP address: 10.1.1.29 Subnet mask: 255.255.0.0	IP address: 192.168.0.29 Subnet mask: 255.255.255.0
Computer30	IP address: 10.1.1.30 Subnet mask: 255.255.0.0	IP address: 192.168.0.30 Subnet mask: 255.255.255.0

Entering Static Internet Protocol (IP) Addressing Information into the Litware Inc. Network Adapter

IMPORTANT   Complete this task from both student computers. This will allow you to configure a static IP address on the Litware Inc. Network adapter. Use the IP addressing information in Table 2-1 to obtain the correct IP address for the Litware Inc. Network adapter.

1. Start your computer running Microsoft Windows Server 2003, and log on as **administrator@*domain*.contoso.com** (where *domain* is the name of your domain).

2. Click Start, and then select Network Connections.

3. Right-click the Litware Inc. Network connection.

4. Select Properties.

5. Highlight Internet Protocol (TCP/IP) in the list of components, and then click Properties.

6. Select the Use The Following IP Address option.

7. Enter the IP addressing information from Table 2-1.

8. Click OK to accept the changes to the Transmission Control Protocol/Internet Protocol (TCP/IP) addressing properties.

9. Click Close to accept the network connection changes.

Installing the DHCP Server Service

> **IMPORTANT**   Complete this task from both student computers. This will allow you to configure your server as a DHCP server.

1. Start your computer running Windows Server 2003, and log on as **administrator@*domain*.contoso.com** (where *domain* is the name of your domain).

2. Click Start, click Administrative Tools, and then click Manage Your Server.

3. In the Manage Your Server window, click Add Or Remove A Role, and then click Next on the Preliminary Steps page of the Configure Your Server Wizard.

4. In the Server Role page, select DHCP Server, and then click Next.

5. On the Summary Of Selections page, click Next.

6. In the New Scope wizard, click Cancel to discontinue creating a scope at this time.

7. In the Cannot Complete page, click Finish to finish installing the DHCP Server service.

Authorizing the DHCP Server Service

> **IMPORTANT**   Complete the task on the computer with the lower number. This will allow you to authorize the server in the Active Directory directory service.

1. Start your computer running Windows Server 2003, and log on as **administrator@*domain*.contoso.com** (where *domain* is the name of your domain).

2. Click Start, and then click Administrative Tools.

3. Right-click DHCP, and select Run As to open the Run As dialog box.

4. In the Run As dialog box fields, enter the following credentials to open the DHCP console:

   a. In the User Box, enter **eadmin@contoso.com**.

   b. In the Password Box, enter **MSPress@LS#1**.

5. Select the name of your server, Computer*xx,* in the DHCP console tree.

6. On the Action menu, select Authorize to authorize the server.

7. To verify that the DHCP server is authorized, in the console tree, press F5.

   The console tree should now display a green arrow signifying that the server is authorized.

Adding and Configuring a DHCP Scope

IMPORTANT *Complete this task from the computer with the lower number. This will allow you to add a DHCP scope for your partner's computer.*

1. Start your computer running Windows Server 2003, and log on as **studentxx@*domain*.contoso.com** (where student*xx* is your student User Name and *domain* is the name of your domain).

2. Click Start, select Control Panel, and then double-click Administrative Tools.

3. Right-click DHCP, and then select Run As to open the Run As dialog box.

4. In the Run As dialog box, select The Following User option, and then enter the following credentials in the dialog box fields to open the DHCP console:

    a. In the User Name box, enter **administrator@*domain*.contoso.com** (where *domain* is the name of your domain).

    b. In the Password box, enter **MSPress@LS#1**.

5. Click OK to open the DHCP console.

6. Select the applicable DHCP server in the console tree.

7. On the Action menu, select New Scope to create a new DHCP scope.

8. In the New Scope wizard, click Next.

9. On the Scope Name page, configure the following:

    a. For the Name option, enter **partner's scope**.

    b. For the Description option, enter **scope for partner's computer**.

10. Click Next.

11. On the IP Address Range page, configure the following:

    a. For the Start IP Address option, enter your partner's Litware Inc. network connection IP address.

    b. For the End IP Address option, enter your partner's Litware Inc. network connection IP address.

    c. For the Subnet Mask option, enter **24** bit or **255.255.255.0**.

12. Click Next.

13. On the Add Exclusions page, click Next.

14. On the Lease Duration page, select 1 Hour, and then click Next.

15. On the Configure DHCP Options page, select No, I Will Configure These Options Later, and then click Next.

16. On the Completing The New Scope Wizard page, click Finish.

Activating a DHCP Scope

IMPORTANT   *Complete this task from the computer with the lower number. This will allow you to activate a DHCP scope.*

1. Start your computer running Windows Server 2003, and log on as **student*xx*@*domain*.contoso.com** (where student*xx* is your student User Name and *domain* is the name of your domain).

2. Click Start, select Control Panel, and then double-click Administrative Tools.

3. Right-click DHCP, and then select Run As to open the Run As dialog box.

4. In the Run As dialog box, select The Following User option, and enter the following credentials in the dialog box fields to open the DHCP console:

   a. In the User Name box, enter **administrator@*domain*.contoso.com** (where *domain* is the name of your domain).

   b. In the Password box, enter **MSPress@LS#1**.

5. Click OK to open the DHCP console.

6. Select and expand the name of your server node in the DHCP console.

7. Select the scope named Partner's Scope.

8. On the Action menu, select Activate.

9. Close the DHCP console.

SCENARIO

You are a network administrator for Contoso, Ltd. You have a Microsoft Windows Server 2003 network that utilizes DHCP for address assignment. There is inconsistency in DHCP's performance, and you have been asked to do an in-depth evaluation of your company's DHCP Server service.

EXERCISE 2-1: BACKING UP AND RESTORING A DHCP DATABASE

Estimated completion time: 10 minutes

You are the network administrator for Contoso. You deployed a DHCP server on the network. After a couple of weeks, Event Viewer logs events that indicate the DHCP Server service may need to be reinstalled. You want to back up the DHCP database and then restore it after the problems are resolved.

Creating a Manual Backup of the DHCP Database

IMPORTANT   *Complete this task from both student computers. This will allow you to create a manual backup of the DHCP database on your server computer.*

1. Start your computer running Windows Server 2003, and log on as **administrator@*domain*.contoso.com** (where *domain* is the name of your domain).

2. Click Start, and then click My Computer.

3. In the My Computer window, double-click the C drive.

4. On the Toolbar menu, select File, select New, and then select Folder.

5. For the name of the folder, type **computer.*xx*** (where computer.*xx* is your assigned computer name).

6. Click Start, and then click Administrative Tools. Click DHCP to open the DHCP console.

7. In the DHCP console tree, select the name of your server.

8. On the Action menu, select Backup.

9. In the Browse For Folder dialog box, select the Computer.*xx* folder (where Computer.*xx* is the name of your assigned computer). You just created this folder on the C drive.

10. Click OK to confirm that a backup of the database will be copied to the Computer.*xx* folder.

Manually Restoring a Backup of the DHCP Database

IMPORTANT   *Complete this task from both student computers. This will allow you to create a manual restore of the DHCP database on your server computer.*

1. Start your computer running Windows Server 2003, and log on as **administrator@*domain*.contoso.com** (where *domain* is the name of your domain).

2. Click Start, click Administrative Tools, and then click DHCP to open the DHCP console.

3. In the DHCP console tree, select the name of your server.

4. On the Action menu, select Restore.

5. In the Browse For Folder dialog box, locate the folder: \Computer.*xx*\New (where Computer.*xx* is the name of your assigned computer).

6. Click Yes to confirm that the DHCP Server service must be stopped and restarted.

QUESTION   *Why does the operating system stop and restart the DHCP Server service when restoring a DHCP database?*

EXERCISE 2-2: COMPACTING THE DHCP DATABASE

Estimated completion time: 10 minutes

You are the network administrator for Contoso. You deployed a DHCP server on the network. After several months, you notice that the DHCP database takes up a good portion of the physical disk. This disk is slowly running out of space, so you decide that you should compact the DHCP database to conserve space.

Compacting a DHCP Database

IMPORTANT   *Complete this task from both student computers. This will allow you to compact the DHCP database on your server computer.*

1. Start your computer running Windows Server 2003, and log on as **administrator@***domain*.**contoso.com** (where *domain* is the name of your domain).

2. Click Start, click Run, and then type **cmd**. Press ENTER.

3. In the command prompt window, type **cd \%systemroot%\ system32\dhcp**, and press ENTER.

4. At the %systemroot%\System32\Dhcp prompt, type **net stop dhcpserver**, and press ENTER.

5. At the %systemroot%\System32\Dhcp prompt, type **jetpack dhcp.mdb tmp.mdb**, and press ENTER.

6. At the %systemroot%\System32\Dhcp prompt, type **net start dhcpserver**, and press ENTER.

7. Close the command prompt window.

QUESTION   *Why do we have to issue a Net Stop command before compacting the database?*

QUESTION   *What is the Tmp.mdb file used for when compacting a DHCP database?*

EXERCISE 2-3: THE DHCP AUDIT LOG

Estimated completion time: 15 minutes

You are the network administrator for Contoso and are responsible for monitoring the DHCP Server service on your network. To facilitate this, you will configure your DHCP server to update statistics every minute and then view the statistics using the DHCP audit logs.

Removing the DHCP Server Service from a Client Computer

IMPORTANT   *Complete these steps from the computer with the higher number. This will allow you to remove the DHCP Server service from your computer.*

1. Start your computer running Windows Server 2003, and log on as **student***xx***@***domain*.**contoso.com** (where student*xx* is your student User Name and *domain* is the name of your domain).

2. Click Start, select Control Panel, and then double-click Administrative Tools.

3. Right-click Manage Your Server, and then select Run As to open the Run As dialog box.

4. In the Run As dialog box, select The Following User option, and enter the following credentials in the dialog box fields to open Manage Your Server:

   a. In the User Name box, enter **administrator@*domain*.contoso.com** (where *domain* is the name of your domain).

   b. In the Password box, enter **MSPress@LS#1**.

5. Click OK to open the Manage Your Server window.

6. Click Add Or Remove A Roll.

7. Click Next on the Preliminary Steps page of the Configure Your Server wizard.

8. On the Server Role page of the Configure Your Server Wizard, select DHCP Server, and then click Next.

9. On the Role Removal Confirmation page, check the Remove The DHCP Server Role check box.

10. Click Next.

11. Click Finish on the DHCP Server Role Removed page.

Creating a Batch File for Testing DHCP Settings

IMPORTANT   Complete this task from the computer with the higher number. This will create a batch file for testing DHCP settings and creating DHCP data.

1. Start your computer running Windows Server 2003, and log on as **student*xx*@*domain*.contoso.com** (where student*xx* is your student User Name and *domain* is the name of your domain).

2. In the Start menu, select All Programs, select Accessories, right-click Command Prompt, and then select Run As to open the Run As dialog box.

3. In the Run As dialog box, select The Following User option, and then enter the following credentials in the dialog box fields to open the command prompt window:

   a. In the User Name box, enter **administrator@*domain*.contoso.com** (where *domain* is the name of your domain).

   b. In the Password box, enter **MSPress@LS#1**.

4. Click OK to open the command prompt window. At the command prompt, type **cd c:**, and then press ENTER, to get to the root of the C drive.

5. At the command prompt, type **notepad dhcptester.bat**, and then press ENTER.

6. Click Yes to indicate you want to create a new file.

7. In Dhcptester.bat – Notepad, type **ipconfig /release**, and then press ENTER. Type **ipconfig /renew**, and then press ENTER.

8. On the Edit menu, choose Select All.

9. On the Edit menu, choose Copy.

10. Press CTRL+V about 20 times to create about 20 copies of the selected text.

11. On the File menu, select Save.

12. On the File menu, select Exit.

Configuring a DHCP Client

IMPORTANT   *Complete this task from the computer with the higher number. This will allow you to configure the student computer as a DHCP client.*

1. Start your computer running Windows Server 2003, and log on as **administrator@*domain*.contoso.com** (where *domain* is the name of your domain).

2. Click Start, and then click Network Connections.

3. Right-click the Litware Inc Network connection icon, and then select Properties.

4. Highlight Internet Protocol (TCP/IP) in the list of components, and then click Properties.

5. Select Obtain An IP Address Automatically.

6. Click OK to accept the changes to the TCP/IP addressing properties.

7. Click Close to accept the network connection changes.

8. Click Start, and then click Run.

9. Type **cmd**, and then press ENTER.

10. In the command prompt window, type **c:\dhcptester.bat**.

IMPORTANT   *The Dhcptester.bat program will execute many Ipconfig /release and /renew commands so that there will be DHCP data logged for the rest of this exercise.*

Configuring DHCP Statistics Update

IMPORTANT   *Complete this task from the computer with the lower number.*

1. Start your computer running Windows Server 2003, and log on as **administrator@*domain*.contoso.com** (where *domain* is the name of your domain).

2. Click Start, click Administrative Tools, and then click DHCP to open the DHCP console.

3. In the DHCP console tree, select the name of your server.

4. On the Action menu, click Properties.

5. In the General tab of the server Properties, enable the Automatically Update Statistics Every setting.

6. In the Minutes option, configure the statistics to update every 1 minute. Click OK.

Viewing the DHCP Audit Log

IMPORTANT   *Complete this task from the computer with the lower number.*

1. Start your computer running Windows Server 2003, and log on as **administrator@***domain***.contoso.com** (where *domain* is the name of your domain).

2. Click Start, and then click My Computer.

3. In the My Computer window, locate the %systemroot%\System32\Dhcp folder.

4. Locate the DHCP audit log. (Hint: It is in the format of DhcpSrvLog*day*.log.)

5. Open the appropriate log file to view the contents of the log file.

6. Note the log entries for the Ipconfig /release and /renew commands that the Dhcptester.bat program executed.

QUESTION   *In the DHCP audit log, what are the headings used to describe operations performed by the DHCP Server service?*

EXERCISE 2-4: MONITORING DHCP PERFORMANCE

Estimated completion time: 20 minutes

You are the network administrator for Contoso. You deployed a DHCP server on the network. Clients receive IP addressing information from the DHCP server, but users report that at times they experience a long delay while logging on and accessing network resources. To decide whether there is a physical layer problem with the network, you must monitor your DHCP server to ensure that clients receive timely and proper IP addressing information.

Configuring DHCP Performance Counters

IMPORTANT   *Complete this task from the computer with the lower number. This will allow you to add performance monitor objects to the System Monitor console.*

1. Start your computer running Windows Server 2003, and log on as **administrator@***domain***.contoso.com** (where *domain* is the name of your domain).

2. Click Start, and then click Administrative Tools.

3. Click Performance to start the Performance Monitor.

4. Delete the counters in the default System Monitor view. (Hint: Click the X on the icon menu bar until it appears dimmed.)

5. Select System Monitor under the Console Root in the window pane on the left side.

6. In the other window pane, click the plus (+) icon to add DHCP Performance Monitor counters.

7. In the Add Counters dialog box, in the Performance Object option, click the drop-down arrow, and then select DHCP Server.

8. Add the following counters by selecting the counter and clicking Add:

   ❑ Acks/sec

   ❑ Packets received/sec

   ❑ Releases/sec

   ❑ Requests/sec

9. After you have added the counters, click Close.

10. Select System Monitor Properties from the icon menu bar or press CTRL+Q.

11. In System Monitor Properties, in the Graph tab, under Vertical Scale and in the Maximum box, type **5**, and then click OK.

12. Click File, and then select Save As to save the Performance console.

13. Click the Desktop icon on the left side, type **dhcp** in the File Name box, and then click Save.

14. Click File, and then select Exit to exit the Performance console.

Using the Dhcptester.bat File to Create DHCP Activity

> **IMPORTANT**   Complete this task from the computer with the higher number. This will allow you to create DHCP activity to view in the Performance console in the next task.

1. Start your computer running Windows Server 2003, and log on as **studentxx@domain.contoso.com** (where studentxx is your student User Name and *domain* is the name of your domain).

2. In the Start menu, select All Programs, select Accessories, right-click Command Prompt, and then select Run As to open the Run As dialog box.

3. In the Run As dialog box, select The Following User option, and enter the following credentials in the dialog box fields to open the command prompt window:

   a. In the User Name box, enter **administrator@domain.contoso.com** (where *domain* is the name of your domain).

   b. In the Password box, enter **MSPress@LS#1**.

4. Click OK to open the command prompt window.

5. In the command prompt window, type **C:\dhcptester.bat**.

Viewing DHCP Activity in the Performance Console

IMPORTANT   *Complete this task as soon after the previous task as possible, from the computer with the lower number. This will allow you to monitor DHCP activity with the Performance console while it occurs.*

1. On the desktop, double-click the DHCP Performance Monitor icon.

2. Select System Monitor in the console tree, and then click the View Report option on the icon menu or press CTRL+R.

   If the values displayed are not changing, the Dhcptester.bat program on the higher-numbered computer has finished running and needs to be run again. See the previous task for instructions.

3. When nonzero values are present, click the Freeze Display icon (the red disc with a white X in the middle) in the icon menu, and record the following values:

   ❑ Acks/sec _____

   ❑ Packets received/sec _____

   ❑ Releases/sec _____

   ❑ Requests/sec _____

EXERCISE 2-5: RESOLVING MISCONFIGURED SERVERS AND CLIENTS

Estimated completion time: 15 minutes

You are the network administrator for Contoso. You just deployed a DHCP server on the Litware Inc. Network. The Litware Inc. Network uses the 192.168.0.0 network address. You configure DHCP server options for client computers on the Litware Inc. Network. However, after you configure the DHCP scope options, clients can access network resources on only the Litware Inc. Network.

Resolving DHCP Server Configuration Errors

IMPORTANT   *Complete this task from the computer with the lower number. This will allow you to configure DHCP server options on the DHCP server computer.*

1. Start your computer running Windows Server 2003, and log on as **administrator@*domain*.contoso.com** (where *domain* is the name of your domain).

2. Click Start, click Administrative Tools, and then click DHCP to open the DHCP console.

3. In the DHCP console tree, select and expand the name of your server node. Select Scope Options.

4. In the Scope pane, click the 003 Router option.

5. On the Action menu, select Properties.

6. Click the Remove button, which is located under the Data Entry section.

7. In the Data entry section under the IP Address heading, enter **10.1.1.100**, click Add, and then click OK.

Checking the DHCP Configuration

IMPORTANT   *Complete the following steps from the computer with the higher number.*

1. Start your computer running Windows Server 2003, and log on as **student*xx*@*domain*.contoso.com** (where student*xx* is your student User Name and *domain* is the name of your domain).

2. In the Start menu, select All Programs, select Accessories, right-click Command Prompt, and select Run As to open the Run As dialog box.

3. In the Run As dialog box, select The Following User option, and enter the following credentials in the dialog box fields to open the command prompt window:

   a. In the User Name box, enter **administrator@*domain*.contoso.com** (where *domain* is the name of your domain).

   b. In the Password box, enter **MSPress@LS#1**.

4. Click OK to open the command prompt window.

5. In the command prompt window, type **ipconfig /release**.

6. In the command prompt window, type **ipconfig /renew**.

7. In the command prompt window, type **ipconfig /all**.

QUESTION   What is the default gateway address given by the DHCP server for the Litware Inc. Network adapter?

QUESTION   What is wrong with this IP address?

Correcting the DHCP Server Configuration

IMPORTANT   *Complete his task from the computer with the lower number. This will allow you to correct the IP address for the 003 Router option on the DHCP server computer.*

1. Start your computer running Windows Server 2003, and log on as **administrator@*domain*.contoso.com** (where *domain* is the name of your domain).

2. Click Start, click Administrative Tools, and then click DHCP to open the DHCP console.

3. In the DHCP console tree, select the name of your server. Expand the console tree to locate Server Options.

4. In the Scope pane, click the 003 Router option.

5. On the Action menu, select Properties.

6. Click the Remove button, which is located under the Data Entry section.

7. In the Data Entry section, under the IP Address heading, enter
   192.168.0.101, click Add, and then click OK.

Checking the DHCP Configuration

IMPORTANT *Complete the following steps from the computer with the higher number.*

1. Start your computer running Windows Server 2003, and log on as
   student*xx*@*domain*.contoso.com (where student*xx* is is your student
   User Name and *domain* is the name of your domain).

2. In the Start menu, select All Programs, select Accessories, right-click Command Prompt, and select Run As to open the Run As dialog box.

3. In the Run As dialog box, select The Following User option, and enter the
   following credentials in the dialog box fields to open the command
   prompt window:

   a. In the User Name box, enter **administrator@*domain*.contoso.com**
      (where *domain* is the name of your domain).

   b. In the Password box, enter **MSPress@LS#1**.

4. Click OK to open the command prompt window.

5. In the command prompt window, type **ipconfig /release**.

6. In the command prompt window, type **ipconfig /renew**.

7. In the command prompt window, type **ipconfig /all**.

QUESTION *What is the default gateway address given by the DHCP server?*

QUESTION *Is this default gateway address possible for the given Litware Inc. Network?*

EXERCISE 2-6: REMOVING DEPENDENCIES BETWEEN LABS

Estimated completion time: 5 minutes

You will now remove the DHCP Server service and configure the Litware Inc.
Network connection on the student computers. This is necessary for the successful
completion of future labs.

Removing the DHCP Server Service

IMPORTANT *Complete these steps from the computer with the lower number. This will allow you to remove the DHCP Server service from your computer.*

1. Start your computer running Windows Server 2003, and log on as **student*xx*@*domain*.contoso.com** (where *domain* is the name of your domain).

2. Click Start, click Administrative Tools, and then click Manage Your Server.

3. In the Manage Your Server window, click Add Or Remove A Role, and then click Next.

4. On the Preliminary Steps page, click Next.

5. On the Server Role page, select DHCP Server, and then click Next.

6. On the Role Removal Confirmation page, select the Remove The DHCP Server Role check box.

7. Click Next to confirm removal of the DHCP Server service.

8. Click Finish to close the Manage Your Server wizard.

Entering Static IP Addressing Information into the Litware Inc. Network Adapter

IMPORTANT   *Complete this task from the computer with the higher number. This will allow you to configure a static IP address on the Litware Inc. Network adapter. Refer to the IP addressing information in Table 2-1 to find the correct IP address for the Litware Inc. Network adapter.*

1. Start your computer running Windows Server 2003, and log on as **administrator@*domain*.contoso.com** (where *domain* is the name of your domain).

2. Click Start, and then select Network Connections.

3. Right-click the Litware Inc Network connection.

4. Select Properties.

5. Highlight Internet Protocol (TCP/IP) in the list of components, and then click Properties.

6. Select the Use The Following IP Address option.

7. Enter the IP addressing information from Table 2-1.

8. Click OK to accept the changes to the Transmission Control Protocol/ Internet Protocol (TCP/IP) addressing properties.

9. Click Close to accept the network connection changes.

LAB REVIEW QUESTIONS

Estimated completion time: 15 minutes

1. What are at least three tools that can be used to monitor DHCP activity?

2. What is the default path for the DHCP audit log?

3. Which tool is used to compact a DHCP database?

4. Why must you stop the DHCP Server service when restoring a DHCP database?

5. When a DHCP client tries to connect to a network, but can't communicate with other computers on the network, what possible solutions could there be?

LAB CHALLENGE 2-1: CREATING A BACKUP STRATEGY FOR CONTOSO

Estimated completion time: 15 minutes

Your supervisor, who is the senior network administrator at Contoso, is concerned about the stability of the network. He has asked you to develop and carry out a backup plan for the DHCP database. He requires you to verify that the automatic backup process works, and he would also like you to complete a manual backup at the end of day each Monday. The manual backup file will be stored on a remote server for added protection against the DHCP server's hardware failure. You have also been asked to ensure that the database is not larger than necessary.

LAB CHALLENGE 2-2: CONFIGURING DYNAMIC UPDATES

Estimated completion time: 20 minutes

You are the network administrator for Litware, Inc. Your network consists of Windows Server 2003 domain controllers and member servers with Microsoft Windows NT 4 clients. You want to migrate all the Windows NT 4 clients to Microsoft Windows XP except for five. You are asked to set up DHCP using secure dynamic updates. You must ensure that the Domain Name System (DNS) is updated for all clients and that the Windows XP clients can update their own host records. Create and implement a solution.

LAB 3

INSTALLING AND CONFIGURING THE DNS SERVER SERVICE

This lab contains the following exercises and activities:

■ Exercise 3-1: Installing the DNS Server Service

■ Exercise 3-2: Creating and Configuring DNS Zones

■ Exercise 3-3: Creating DNS Records

■ Exercise 3-4: Configuring Forwarding

■ Lab Review Questions

■ Lab Challenge 3-1: Configuring DNS

After completing this lab, you will be able to

■ Install the DNS Server service.

■ Create and configure forward and reverse lookup DNS zones.

■ Create DNS records.

■ Configure DNS forwarding.

Estimated completion time: 105 minutes

SCENARIO

You are the network administrator of an organization. Your organization currently wants to install Domain Name System (DNS) servers in each of the child domains to prevent unnecessary DNS traffic across your wide area network (WAN) links. You must configure the DNS subdomains with forward and reverse lookup zones and create DNS records within each DNS subdomain. You must also configure your DNS server to forward DNS requests for the contoso.com domain to a DNS server that is authoritative for the contoso.com domain.

EXERCISE 3-1: INSTALLING THE DNS SERVER SERVICE

Estimated completion time: 10 minutes

You are the network administrator for Contoso and have been asked to configure your network servers to perform name resolution. First, you must install the DNS Server service for it to host DNS records for your subdomain. After you have installed DNS, you will configure your DNS zones and configure your name servers to perform conditional forwarding.

Installing DNS

> **IMPORTANT**   Complete this task on both student computers. This will allow you to install the DNS Server service on your computer.

1. Start your computer running Microsoft Windows Server 2003 and log on as **student*xx*@*domain*.contoso.com** (where student*xx* is your student User Name and *domain* is the name of your domain).

2. Click Start, and then click Control Panel.

3. While holding down the Shift key, right-click the Add Or Remove Programs option, and then click Run As to open the Run As dialog box.

4. In the Run As dialog box, select The Following User option, and then enter the following credentials in the dialog box fields to open the Add Or Remove Programs wizard:

   a. In the User Name box, enter **administrator@*domain*.contoso.com** (where *domain* is the name of your domain).

   b. In the Password box, enter **MSPress@LS#1**.

5. Click OK to open the Add Or Remove Programs wizard.

6. In the Add Or Remove Programs wizard, click the Add/Remove Windows Components icon on the left, highlight Networking Services, and then click Details.

7. In the Networking Services dialog box, check the Domain Name System (DNS) check box, and then click OK.

8. In the Windows Components wizard, click Next.

9. When the configuration process is complete, click Finish and close all open windows.

> **QUESTION**   What are the three nodes created directly under the DNS server in the DNS Management console?

Verifying the Primary DNS Suffix

> **IMPORTANT**   Complete this task on both student computers. This will allow you to verify the primary DNS suffix for your computer. For DNS to create the correct name server (NS) and host name (A) records when you create the forward lookup zone for your domain, the primary DNS suffix must be configured correctly.

1. Start your computer running Windows Server 2003, and log on as
   student*xx*@*domain*.contoso.com (where student*xx* is your student
   User Name and *domain* is the name of your domain).

2. Click Start, and then click Control Panel to open the Control Panel.

3. Press the Shift key and right-click the System icon, and then click Run As
   to open the Run As dialog box.

4. Select The Following User option, and then enter the following credentials
   in the dialog box fields to open the System Properties window:

   a. In the User Name box, enter **administrator@*domain*.contoso.com**.

   b. In the Password box, enter **MSPress@LS#1**.

5. Click OK to open the System Properties window.

6. In the System Properties window, click the Computer Name tab.

7. To open the Computer Name Changes window, click Change.

8. When you are prompted with the Computer Name Changes dialog box,
   click OK to continue renaming this domain controller.

9. In the Computer Name Changes dialog box, click More to open the DNS
   Suffix And NetBIOS Computer Name window.

10. In the DNS Suffix And NetBIOS Computer Name window, in the Primary
    DNS Suffix Of This Computer box, verify the appropriate child domain
    name from Table 3-1. (For example, atlanta.contoso.com.)

11. Record the Primary DNS Suffix of your computer:

    _____

12. Click Cancel to close the DNS Suffix And NetBIOS Computer Name
    dialog box.

13. Click Cancel to close the Computer Name Changes dialog box.

14. Click Cancel to close the System Properties dialog box.

EXERCISE 3-2: CREATING AND CONFIGURING DNS ZONES

Estimated completion time: 25 minutes

Now that you have installed DNS for your subdomain, you must create the lookup
zones that will be used to host the DNS records for your subdomain.

Creating a Standard Primary DNS Forward Lookup Zone

> **IMPORTANT**   Complete this task from the computer with the lower number. This will
> allow you to create a Standard Primary DNS Forward Lookup zone on your server.

1. Start your computer running Windows Server 2003, and log on as
   student*xx*@*domain*.contoso.com (where student*xx* is your student
   User Name and *domain* is the name of your domain).

2. Click Start, select Control Panel, and then double-click Administrative Tools.

3. Right-click DNS, and then click Run As to open the Run As dialog box.

4. In the Run As dialog box, select The Following User option, and then enter the following credentials in the dialog box fields to open the DNS console:

   a. In the User Name box, enter **administrator@*domain*.contoso.com**.

   b. In the Password box, enter **MSPress@LS#1**.

5. Click OK to open the DNS console.

6. In the DNS console tree, expand the name of your server node, Computer*xx*.

   QUESTION   What DNS forward lookup zones are created after the DNS Server service is installed?

7. Select and right-click Forward Lookup Zones, and then select New Zone.

8. On the Welcome To The New Zone Wizard page, click Next.

9. On the Zone Type page, verify that Primary Zone is selected.

10. Clear the Store The Zone In Active Directory (Available Only If DNS Server Is A Domain Controller) check box, and then click Next.

11. On the Zone Name page, in the Zone Name box, type ***domain*.contoso.com** (where *domain* is the name of your domain), and then click Next.

12. On the Zone File page, verify that Create A New File With This File Name is selected, and then click Next.

13. On the Dynamic Update page, verify that Do Not Allow Dynamic Updates is selected, and then click Next.

14. On the Completing The New Zone Wizard page, click Finish.

Adding a Name Server to Your Forward Lookup Zone

IMPORTANT   Complete this task from the computer with the lower number. This will allow you to add your partner's computer as a name server in the domain.contoso.com forward lookup zone.

1. Start your computer running Windows Server 2003, and log on as **student*xx*@*domain*.contoso.com** (where student*xx* is your student User Name and *domain* is the name of your domain).

2. Click Start, select Control Panel, and then double-click Administrative Tools.

3. Right-click DNS, and then click Run As to open the Run As dialog box.

4. In the Run As dialog box, select The Following User option, and then enter the following credentials in the dialog box fields to open the DNS console:

   a. In the User Name box, enter **administrator@*domain*.contoso.com**.

   b. In the Password box, enter **MSPress@LS#1**.

5. Click OK to open the DNS console.

6. In the console tree, expand the name of your server, expand Forward Lookup Zones, select and right-click *Domain*.Contoso.Com, and then click Properties.

7. In the *Domain*.Contoso.Com Properties page, in the Name Servers tab, click Add.

8. In the Server Fully Qualified Domain Name (FQDN) box of the New Resource Record dialog box, type the FQDN of your partner's computer. In the IP Address box, type your partner's IP address, click Add, and then click OK.

9. Click OK to close the *Domain*.Contoso.Com Properties dialog box.

Creating a Stub Zone and Verifying Zone Transfer Settings

IMPORTANT   Complete this task from the computer with the lower number. This will allow you to create a stub zone where your instructor's computer is the master. It will verify that the *domain.contoso.com* forward lookup zone is set to allow zone transfers.

1. Start your computer running Windows Server 2003, and log on as **student*xx*@*domain*.contoso.com**. (where student*xx* is your student User Name and *domain* is the name of your domain).

2. Click Start, select Control Panel, and then double-click Administrative Tools.

3. Right-click DNS, and then click Run As to open the Run As dialog box.

4. In the Run As dialog box, select The Following User option, and then enter the following credentials in the dialog box fields to open the DNS console:

    a. In the User Name box, enter **administrator@*domain*.contoso.com**.

    b. In the Password box, enter **MSPress@LS#1**.

5. Click OK to open the DNS console.

6. In the DNS console tree, expand the name of your server, and then select and right-click Forward Lookup Zones. Select New Zone.

7. On the Welcome To The New Zone Wizard page, click Next.

8. On the Zone Type page, click Stub Zone.

9. Clear the Store The Zone In Active Directory (Available Only If DNS Server Is A Domain Controller) check box, and then click Next.

10. On the Zone Name page, type **contoso.com**, and then click Next.

11. On the Zone File page, verify that Create A New File With This File Name is selected, and then click Next.

12. In the IP Address box on the Master DNS Servers page, type the instructor's computer IP address (10.1.1.200), click Add, and then click Next.

13. On the Completing The New Zone Wizard page, click Finish.

14. In the DNS console tree, expand Forward Lookup Zones, select and right-click *Domain*.Contoso.Com, and then select Properties.

15. On the *Domain*.Contoso.Com Properties page, click the Zone Transfer tab, and then verify that Allow Zone Transfers is selected.

16. Click OK.

Creating a Standard Secondary DNS Zone

IMPORTANT   *Complete this task from the computer with the higher number. This will allow you to create a standard secondary forward lookup zone for your subdomain using your partner's DNS server as the master.*

1. Start your computer running Windows Server 2003, and log on as **student*xx*@*domain*.contoso.com** (where student*xx* is your student User Name and *domain* is the name of your domain).

2. Click Start, select Control Panel, and then double-click Administrative Tools.

3. Right-click DNS, and then click Run As to open the Run As dialog box.

4. Select The Following User option, and then enter the following credentials in the dialog box fields to open the DNS console:

   a. In the User Name box, enter **administrator@*domain*.contoso.com**.

   b. In the Password box, enter **MSPress@LS#1**.

5. Click OK to open the DNS console.

6. In the DNS console tree, expand your computer name.

7. Select and right-click Forward Lookup Zones, and then select New Zone.

8. On the Welcome To The New Zone Wizard page, click Next.

9. On the Zone Type page, select the Secondary Zone option, and then click Next.

10. On the Zone Name page in the Zone Name box, type *domain*.**contoso.com** (where *domain* is the name of your domain), and then click Next.

11. In the IP Address box on the Master DNS Servers page, type your partner's IP address, click Add, and then click Next.

12. On the Completing The New Zone Wizard page, click Finish.

Creating a DNS Reverse Lookup Zone

IMPORTANT   *Complete this task from the computer with the lower number. This will allow you to create a standard primary reverse lookup zone for your subnet.*

1. Start your computer running Windows Server 2003, and log on as **student*xx*@*domain*.contoso.com** (where student*xx* is your student User Name and *domain* is the name of your domain).

2. Click Start, select Control Panel, and then double-click Administrative Tools.

3. Right-click DNS, and then click Run As to open the Run As dialog box.

4. Select The Following User option, and then enter the following credentials in the dialog box fields to open the DNS console:

    a. In the User Name box, enter **administrator@*domain*.contoso.com**.

    b. In the Password box, enter **MSPress@LS#1**.

5. Click OK to open the DNS console.

6. In the DNS console tree, expand *Server*, and then click Reverse Lookup Zones.

7. Select and right-click Reverse Lookup Zones, and then click New Zone.

8. On the Welcome to the New Zone Wizard page, click Next.

9. On the Zone Type page, click Primary Zone, clear the Store The Zone In Active Directory (Available Only If DNS Server Is A Domain Controller) check box, and then click Next.

10. In the Network ID box on the Reverse Lookup Zone Name page, type the first three octets of your IP address (For example, for an IP address of 10.1.1.1, type **10.1.1**.), and then click Next.

11. On the Zone File page, click Next to accept the default settings.

12. On the Dynamic Update page, click Next to accept the default settings.

13. On the Completing The New Zone Wizard page, click Finish.

14. Close the DNS console.

> **QUESTION**   Which types of DNS zone records are listed in the reverse lookup zone file?

> **QUESTION**   What other types of DNS zone records are created in the reverse lookup zone file?

Configuring DNS Adapter Settings

> **IMPORTANT**   Complete this task from the computer with the lower number. This will allow you to configure the Contoso Ltd Network adapter with the DNS server IP address of your computer. Your server therefore becomes a DNS client of the DNS Server service on your computer.

1. Start your computer running Windows Server 2003, and log on as **administrator@*domain*.contoso.com** (where *domain* is the name of your domain).

2. Click Start, and then click Network Connections to open the Network Connections window.

3. Right-click the Contoso Ltd Network connection icon, and then click Properties.

4. In the Contoso Ltd Network Properties window, click Internet Protocol (TCP/IP), and then click Properties.

5. In the Internet Protocol (TCP/IP) Properties dialog box, verify that the Use The Following DNS Server Addresses option is selected, type your assigned IP address in the Preferred DNS Server box, and then click OK.

6. Click Close to close the Contoso Ltd Network Properties dialog box.

7. Close all open windows.

IMPORTANT   Complete the following tasks from the computer with the higher number. This will allow you to configure your Contoso Ltd Network adapter with a DNS server IP address of your partner's computer. Your server therefore becomes a DNS client of the DNS Server service on your partner's computer.

1. Start your computer running Windows Server 2003, and log on as **administrator@*domain*.contoso.com** (where *domain* is the name of your domain).

2. Click Start, and then click Network Connections to open the Network Connections window.

3. Right-click the Contoso Ltd Network connection icon, and then click Properties.

4. In the Contoso Ltd Network Properties window, click Internet Protocol (TCP/IP), and then click Properties.

5. In the Internet Protocol (TCP/IP) Properties dialog box, verify that the Use The Following DNS Server Addresses option is selected, type your partner's assigned IP address in the Preferred DNS Server box, and then click OK.

6. Click Close to close the Contoso Ltd Network Properties dialog box.

7. Close all open windows.

Enabling Dynamic Updates

IMPORTANT   Complete this task from the computer with the lower number. You must now enable dynamic updates on your subdomain's forward lookup zone.

1. Start your computer running Windows Server 2003, and log on as **student*x.x*@*domain*.contoso.com** (where student*x.x* is your student User Name and *domain* is the name of your domain).

2. Click Start, select Control Panel, and then double-click Administrative Tools.

3. Right-click DNS, and then click Run As to open the Run As dialog box.

4. In the Run As dialog box, select The Following User option, and then enter the following credentials in the dialog box fields to open the DNS console:

   a. In the User Name box, enter **administrator@domain.contoso.com**.

   b. In the Password box, enter **MSPress@LS#1**.

5. Click OK to open the DNS console.

6. In the console tree, expand Computer*xx* (where Computer*xx* is the name of your computer).

7. Expand Forward Lookup Zones, select and right-click *Domain*.Contoso.Com, and then click Properties.

8. On the *Domain*.Contoso.Com Properties page, in the General tab under Dynamic Updates, click the drop-down arrow, and then select Nonsecure And Secure.

9. Click OK to close the *Domain*.Contoso.Com Properties dialog box.

10. Close the DNS Management console.

QUESTION   How do dynamic updates reduce the administrative overhead associated with DNS administration?

Converting to Active Directory–Integrated Zones

IMPORTANT   *Complete this task from the computer with the lower number. This will allow you to change the standard primary zones to Active Directory–integrated zones.*

1. Start your computer running Windows Server 2003, and log on as **student*xx*@*domain*.contoso.com** (where student*xx* is your student User Name and *domain* is the name of your domain).

2. Click Start, select Control Panel, and then double-click Administrative Tools.

3. Right-click DNS, and then click Run As to open the Run As dialog box.

4. Select The Following User option, and then enter the following credentials in the dialog box fields to open the DNS console:

    a. In the User Name box, enter **administrator@*domain*.contoso.com**.

    b. In the Password box, enter **MSPress@LS#1**.

5. Click OK to open the DNS console.

QUESTION   What is the one requirement needed to convert a standard primary DNS zone to an Active Directory–integrated zone?

6. In the DNS console tree, expand your computer name, expand Forward Lookup Zones, select and right-click *Domain*.Contoso.Com, and then click Properties.

7. In the General tab, click Change.

8. On the Change Zone Type page, check the Store The Zone In Active Directory (Available Only If DNS Server Is A Domain Controller) check box, and then click OK.

9. Click OK to close the *Domain*.Contoso.Com Properties window.

10. Close the DNS Management console.

IMPORTANT   *Complete the following tasks from the computer with the higher number. This allows you to convert the standard secondary zones to Active Directory–integrated zones.*

1. Start your computer running Windows Server 2003, and log on as **studentxx@domain.contoso.com** (where studentxx is your student User Name and *domain* is the name of your domain).

2. Click Start, select Control Panel, and then double-click Administrative Tools.

3. Right-click DNS, and then click Run As to open the Run As dialog box.

4. Select The Following User option, and then enter the following credentials in the dialog box fields to open the DNS console:

   a. In the User Name box, enter **administrator@domain.contoso.com**.

   b. In the Password box, enter **MSPress@LS#1**.

5. Click OK to open the DNS console.

6. In the console tree, expand your computer name, expand Forward Lookup Zones, select and right-click *Domain*.Contoso.Com, and then click Properties.

7. In the General tab, click Change.

8. On the Change Zone Type page, select Primary Zone, and check the Store The Zone In Active Directory (Available Only If DNS Server Is A Domain Controller) check box, and then click OK.

9. Click OK to close the *Domain*.Contoso.Com Properties window.

10. Click Yes when asked if you want this zone to become an active directory integrated zone.

11. In the Active Directory Service Warning, click Yes to accept the default.

12. In the DNS warning, click OK.

13. Close the DNS Management console.

EXERCISE 3-3: CREATING DNS RECORDS

Estimated completion time: 15 minutes

After you have created the appropriate DNS lookup zones, you might have to create different types of records within the lookup zones.

Creating a Host Record

IMPORTANT   *Complete this task from the computer with the lower number. This will allow you to create DNS host records on the DNS server computer.*

1. Start your computer running Windows Server 2003, and log on as **studentxx@domain.contoso.com** (where studentxx is your student User Name and *domain* is the name of your domain).

2. Click Start, select Control Panel, and then double-click Administrative Tools.

3. Right-click DNS, and then click Run As to open the Run As dialog box.

4. Select The Following User option, and then enter the following credentials in the dialog box fields to open the DNS console:

    a. In the User Name box, enter **administrator@*domain*.contoso.com**.

    b. In the Password box, enter **MSPress@LS#1**.

5. Click OK to open the DNS console.

6. In the DNS console tree, expand Forward Lookup Zones, and then expand *Domain*.Contoso.Com.

7. Select and right-click the *Domain*.Contoso.Com domain, and then click New Host (A).

8. In the Name (Uses Parent Domain Name If Blank) box, type **hostrecord**.

9. In the IP Address box, type your computer's IP address, and then click Add Host.

10. In the DNS dialog box that states the host record was successfully created, click OK.

11. Click Done in the New Host dialog box.

12. Close the DNS Management console.

Verifying a Host Record

> **IMPORTANT**   Complete this task from both student computers. This will allow you to verify DNS records on the DNS server computer.

1. Start your computer running Windows Server 2003, and log on as **student*xx*@*domain*.contoso.com** (where student*xx* is your student User Name and *domain* is the name of your domain).

2. Click Start, click Run, and then type **cmd**.

3. At the command-line prompt, type **nslookup hostrecord**.

> **QUESTION**   What is the address of host record?

4. Close the command prompt window.

Creating a CNAME Record

> **IMPORTANT**   Complete this task from the computer with the lower number. This will allow you to create DNS canonical name (CNAME) records on the DNS server computer.

1. Start your computer running Windows Server 2003, and log on as **student*xx*@*domain*.contoso.com** (where student*xx* is your student User Name and *domain* is the name of your domain).

2. Click Start, select Control Panel, and then double-click Administrative Tools.

3. Right-click DNS, and then click Run As to open the Run As dialog box.

4. Select The Following User option, and then enter the following credentials in the dialog box fields to open the DNS console:

   a. In the User Name box, enter **administrator@domain.contoso.com**.

   b. In the Password box, enter **MSPress@LS#1**.

5. Click OK to open the DNS console.

6. In the DNS console tree, expand Forward Lookup Zones and *Domain*.Contoso.Com.

7. Select and right-click the *Domain*.Contoso.Com domain, and then click New Alias (CNAME).

8. In the New Resource Record dialog box, in the Alias Name (Uses Parent Domain Name If Blank) box, type **cnamerecord**.

9. In the Fully Qualified Domain Name (FQDN) For Target Host box, type **computer*xx*.*domain*.contoso.com** (where computer*xx* is your assigned computer name and *domain* is your assigned domain).

10. Click OK.

11. Close the DNS Management console.

Verifying a Host Record

IMPORTANT   Complete this task from both student computers. This will allow you to verify DNS CNAME records on the DNS server computer.

1. Start your computer running Windows Server 2003, and log on as **student*xx*@*domain*.contoso.com** (where student*xx* is your student User Name and *domain* is the name of your domain).

2. Click Start, click Run, and then type **cmd**.

3. In the command-line prompt, type **nslookup cnamerecord**.

   QUESTION   What is the address of the CNAME record?

   QUESTION   By which host name is the CNAME record also known?

4. Close the command prompt window.

EXERCISE 3-4: CONFIGURING FORWARDING

Estimated completion time: 10 minutes

You have now installed and configured the DNS zones to hold DNS records. These records are used to resolve host names to IP addresses. Clients in your DNS subdomain might also need to locate other hosts, including those on the Internet. If this is the case, you must configure your DNS server to forward requests to another DNS server computer.

IMPORTANT   This exercise requires that you have Internet connectivity configured for the classroom and an Internet DNS server's IP address to use.

Testing DNS Resolution Outside the Internal Network

IMPORTANT   Complete this task from the computer with the higher number. This will illustrate that forwarding is necessary to access resources outside of the internal network.

1. Start your computer running Windows Server 2003, and log on as **studentxx@domain.contoso.com** (where studentxx is your student User Name and *domain* is the name of your domain).

2. Click Start, click Run, and then type **cmd**.

3. In the command-line prompt, type **nslookup microsoft.com**.

   QUESTION   What is the response from Nslookup?

Configuring Conditional Forwarding

IMPORTANT   Complete this task from the computer with the lower number. This will allow you to configure conditional forwarding on your DNS server.

1. Start your computer running Windows Server 2003, and log on as **studentxx@domain.contoso.com** (where studentxx is your student User Name and *domain* is the name of your domain).

2. Click Start, select Control Panel, and then double-click Administrative Tools.

3. Right-click DNS, and then click Run As to open the Run As dialog box.

4. Select The Following User option, and then enter the following credentials in the dialog box fields to open the DNS console:

   a. In the User Name box, enter **administrator@domain.contoso.com**.

   b. In the Password box, enter **MSPress@LS#1**.

5. Click OK to open the DNS console.

6. In the DNS console tree, select and right-click your computer name, and then click Properties.

7. On the server properties page, in the Forwarders tab, click New, and in the DNS Domain box, type **microsoft.com**, and then click OK.

8. In the server properties page, in the Selected Domain's Forwarder IP Address List box, type a DNS server's IP address that is assigned by the instructor. (This DNS server must be an Internet service provider's [ISP's] or that of another DNS server that is external to the classroom.)

9. Click Add to add the IP address to the IP Address list.

10. Click OK to accept the changes to conditional forwarding.

11. Close all windows.

Testing DNS Resolution Outside the Internal Network

IMPORTANT   *Complete this task from the computer with the higher number. This will illustrate that forwarding has allowed access to resources outside the internal network.*

1. Start your computer running Windows Server 2003, and log on as **student*xx*@*domain*.contoso.com** (where student*xx* is your student User Name and *domain* is the name of your domain).

2. Click Start, click Run, and then type **cmd**.

3. In the command-line prompt, type **nslookup microsoft.com**.

QUESTION   *What is the response from Nslookup?*

LAB REVIEW QUESTIONS

Estimated completion time: 15 minutes

1. What TCP/IP setting must be configured before installing the DNS Server service?

2. Why must you create a stub zone for the contoso.com domain on your DNS server?

3. You want to have only secure dynamic updates for a DNS zone file. Which type of zone file must you have?

4. When do you use forwarding with DNS? Give one example.

5. What is the difference between forwarding and conditional forwarding?

LAB CHALLENGE 3-1: CONFIGURING DNS

Estimated completion time: 30 minutes

You and your partner are network administrators for the *domain*.contoso.com. You have been asked to configure DNS for your network. After evaluating your network, you determine that one standard primary and one standard secondary server will meet the name resolution requirements of your network. You do not want your DNS servers to resolve external names, but would like your DNS servers to use the instructor's computer for external name resolution. All of your client computers run Microsoft Windows XP and should be able to update their own host records. Dynamic Host Configuration Protocol (DHCP) should update all PTR records. How should you go about implementing your solution for your domain?

LAB 4

MANAGING AND MONITORING DNS

This lab contains the following exercises and activities:

- Exercise 4-1: Preliminary Tasks
- Exercise 4-2: Manually Replicating a DNS Zone
- Exercise 4-3: Monitoring and Troubleshooting DNS
- Exercise 4-4: Managing DNS
- Exercise 4-5: Securing DNS
- Exercise 4-6: Removing the DNS Server Service
- Lab Review Questions
- Lab Challenge 4-1: Installing and Managing DNS

After completing this lab, you will be able to:

- Install the Microsoft Windows Server 2003 Support Tools.
- Monitor the Domain Name System (DNS) Server service.
- Troubleshoot the DNS Server service.
- Manage the DNS Server service.
- Secure a DNS server.

Estimated completion time: 125 minutes (This estimate includes the Before You Begin setup procedures.)

BEFORE YOU BEGIN

Estimated completion time: 10 minutes

> **IMPORTANT**   If you have not completed the exercises in Lab 3, "Installing and Configuring the DNS Server Service," you must complete the following prerequisite procedures.

Installing the DNS Server Service

> **IMPORTANT**   Complete this task on both student computers. This will allow you to install the DNS Server service on your computers. After you have installed the DNS Server service, you will configure an Active Directory–integrated DNS zone.

1. Start your computer running Windows Server 2003, and log on as **studentxx@domain.contoso.com** where studentxx is your student User Name and *domain* is the name of your domain.

2. Click Start, and then click Control Panel.

3. While holding down the Shift key, right-click the Add Or Remove Programs option, and then click Run As to open the Run As dialog box.

4. In the Run As dialog box, select The Following User option, and then enter the following credentials in the dialog box fields to open the Add Or Remove Programs window:

    a. In the User Name box, enter **administrator@domain.contoso.com**.

    b. In the Password box, enter **MSPress@LS#1**.

5. Click OK to open the Add Or Remove Programs window.

6. In the Add Or Remove Programs window, click Add/Remove Windows Components.

7. In the Windows Components wizard, on the Windows Components page, under Components, click Networking Services, and then click Details.

8. In the Networking Services dialog box, select the Domain Name System (DNS) check box, and then click OK.

9. In the Windows Components wizard, click Next.

10. If prompted for the Windows Server 2003 installation files, place the Windows Server 2003 installation CD into the CD-ROM drive, and then click OK.

11. When the configuration process is complete, click Finish, and then close all open windows.

Creating and Configuring an Active Directory–Integrated DNS Zone

> **IMPORTANT**   Complete this task from the computer with the lower number. This will allow you to create a forward lookup zone for your domain. The zone should automatically be replicated on the higher numbered computer within minutes.

1. Start your computer running Windows Server 2003, and log on as **student*xx*@*domain*.contoso.com** where student*xx* is your student User Name and *domain* is the name of your domain.

2. Click Start, click Control Panel, and then double-click Administrative Tools.

3. Right-click DNS, and then select Run As to open the Run As dialog box.

4. In the Run As dialog box, select The Following User option, and enter the following credentials in the dialog box fields to open the DNS console:

   a. In the User Name box, enter **administrator@*domain*.contoso.com** where *domain* is the name of your domain.

   b. In the Password box, enter **MSPress@LS#1**.

5. Click OK to open the DNS console.

6. In the DNS console tree, expand Computer*xx*, and then click Forward Lookup Zones.

7. Right-click Forward Lookup Zones, and then click New Zone.

8. On the Welcome To The New Zone Wizard page, click Next.

9. On the Zone Type page, verify that the Primary Zone and the Store The Zone In Active Directory (Available If The DNS Server Is A Domain Controller) options are selected, and then click Next.

10. On the Active Directory Zone Replication Scope page, verify that the To All Domain Controllers In The Active Directory Domain *domain*.contoso.com option is selected where *domain* is the name of your domain, and then click Next.

11. Type **domain.contoso.com** in the Zone Name box where *domain* is the name of your domain, and then click Next.

12. On the Dynamic Update page, verify that the Allow Only Secure Dynamic Updates (Recommended For Active Directory) option is selected, and then click Next.

13. On the Completing The New Zone Wizard page, click Finish.

14. Expand Forward Lookup Zones.

15. Select and right-click **Domain.Contoso.Com**, and then select properties.

16. In the server Properties page, in the Zone Transfers tab, select Allow Zone Transfers, and then select To Any Server. Click OK.

17. Close all open windows.

SCENARIO

You are the network administrator for Blue Yonder Airlines. You have deployed several DNS servers and Active Directory domain controllers on your company network. Each DNS server is running Active Directory–integrated zones. Management has requested that you ensure DNS services are operating efficiently and securely. You must manage, monitor, and secure the DNS servers that are operating on the network. You will use the support tools that are located on the Microsoft Windows Server 2003 CD in addition to the management and monitoring tools that are built in to DNS.

EXERCISE 4-1: PRELIMINARY TASKS

Estimated completion time: 5 minutes

In this exercise, you will configure settings and add tools in preparation for the rest of the lab. These tools are used to monitor and troubleshoot the DNS Server service.

Installing Windows Server 2003 Support Tools

IMPORTANT Complete this task from both student computers. This will allow you to install the Windows Server 2003 Support Tools on your student computer.

1. Start your computer running Windows Server 2003, and log on as **administrator@***domain*.**contoso.com** where *domain* is the name of your domain.

2. Click Start, and then click My Computer.

3. In the My Computer window, right-click the drive that represents your CD-ROM drive, and then click Open (your Microsoft Windows Server 2003 Installation CD should be in the CD-ROM drive).

4. Open the Support folder, and then the Tools folder, and then double-click SUPTOOLS.MSI.

5. In the Windows Support Tools Setup Wizard window, click Next.

6. On the End User License Agreement page, review the license agreement and then click I Agree if you agree with the terms. (If you do not agree with the terms, you cannot continue with this installation.) Click Next.

7. On the User Information page, accept the default name and organization, and then click Next to continue.

8. On the Destination Directory page, click Install Now to begin the installation.

9. On the Completing The Windows Support Tools Setup Wizard page, click Finish to complete the installation of the Windows Support Tools.

10. Close all open windows.

Configuring DNS Adapter Settings

IMPORTANT Complete this task from both student computers. This will allow you to configure the network adapter that is connected to the Contoso Ltd. Network to use your instructor's computer's DNS Server service.

1. Start your computer running Windows Server 2003, and log on as **administrator@***domain*.**contoso.com** where *domain* is the name of your domain.

2. Click Start, and then click Network Connections to open the Network Connections window.

3. Right-click the Contoso Ltd Network connection icon, and then click Properties.

4. Click Internet Protocol (TCP/IP), and then click Properties.

5. On the Internet Protocol (TCP/IP) Properties page, verify that Use The Following DNS Server Addresses option is selected, then type the IP address of your instructor's computer (**10.1.1.200**) in the Preferred DNS Server box, and then click OK.

6. Ensure that there is no entry in the Default Gateway box, and that there is no entry in the Alternate DNS Server box.

7. Click Close to close the Contoso Ltd Network Properties page.

8. Close all open windows.

EXERCISE 4-2: MANUALLY REPLICATING A DNS ZONE

Estimated completion time: 10 minutes

In this exercise, you manually replicate DNS zone information. This is not normally required, because Active Directory–integrated DNS zone replication is also included with the normal Active Directory replication, but there are times when the DNS zone information might need to be manually replicated, such as when you manually create DNS records and must have the DNS host immediately accessible.

Manually Creating a Host Record

IMPORTANT *Complete this task from the student computer with the lower number. This will allow you to create a new host record in the DNS forward lookup zone.*

1. Start your computer running Windows Server 2003, and log on as **student*xx*@*domain*.contoso.com** where student*xx* is your student User Name and *domain* is the name of your domain.

2. Click Start, click Control Panel, and then double-click Administrative Tools.

3. Right-click DNS, and then select Run As to open the Run As dialog box.

4. In the Run As dialog box, select The Following User option, and then enter the following credentials in the dialog box fields to open the DNS console:

   a. In the User Name box, enter **administrator@*domain*.contoso.com** where *domain* is the name of your domain.

   b. In the Password field, enter **MSPress@LS#1**.

5. Click OK to open the DNS console.

6. In the DNS console tree, expand Computer.*xx* where Computer.*xx* is the name of your computer, expand Forward Lookup Zones, and then select *Domain*.Contoso.Com.

7. Right-click the *Domain*.Contoso.Com domain, and then click New Host (A).

8. In the Name (Uses Parent Domain Name If Blank) box, type **newhost**.

9. In the IP Address box, type the IP address of your computer, and then click Add Host.

10. Click OK on the confirmation that the record was successfully created.

11. Click Done.

12. Close the DNS Management console, and close all open windows.

Manually Replicating a DNS Zone Using the Active Directory Sites And Services Snap-In

IMPORTANT   *Complete this task from the student computer with the higher number. This will allow you to replicate the information contained in the Active Directory database.*

1. Start your computer running Windows Server 2003, and log on as **student*xx*@*domain*.contoso.com** where student*xx* is your student User Name and *domain* is the name of your domain.

2. Click Start, click Control Panel, and then double-click Administrative Tools.

3. Right-click Active Directory Sites And Services, and then select Run As to open the Run As dialog box.

4. In the Run As dialog box, select The Following User option, and then enter the following credentials in the dialog box fields to open the Active Directory Sites And Services console:

    a. In the User Name box, enter **administrator@*domain*.contoso.com** where *domain* is the name of your domain.

    b. In the Password box, enter **MSPress@LS#1**.

5. Click OK to open the Active Directory Sites And Services console.

6. In the Active Directory Sites And Services console tree, expand Sites, and then expand Default-First-Site-Name.

7. In the Active Directory Sites And Services console tree, expand Servers, and then expand Computer.*xx* where Computer.*xx* is the name of your computer, and then select NTDS Settings.

8. In the Active Directory Sites And Services scope pane, right-click each of the <automatically generated> connection objects, and then select Replicate Now, and then click OK in the Replicate Now dialog box.

9. Close the Active Directory Sites And Services console window, and close all open windows.

Verifying Replication and Allowing Zone Transfers

IMPORTANT *Complete this task from the student computer with the higher number. This will allow you to see that the new host record has been replicated into the DNS forward lookup zone. You will also configure the zone domain.contoso.com to allow zone transfers, in preparation for future tasks.*

1. Start your computer running Windows Server 2003, and log on as **studentxx@domain.contoso.com** where studentxx is your student User Name and *domain* is the name of your domain.

2. Click Start, click Control Panel, and then double-click Administrative Tools.

3. Right-click DNS, and select Run As to open the Run As dialog box.

4. In the Run As dialog box, select The Following User option, and enter the following credentials in the dialog box fields to open the DNS console:

   a. In the User Name box, enter **administrator@domain.contoso.com** where *domain* is the name of your domain.

   b. In the Password box, enter **MSPress@LS#1**.

5. Click OK to open the DNS console.

6. In the DNS console tree, expand Computer*xx* where Computer*xx* is the name of your computer, expand Forward Lookup Zones, and select *Domain*.Contoso.Com where *Domain*.Contoso.Com is the name of your domain.

7. In the DNS console scope pane, verify that the host record (newhost) appears in the window.

8. Right-click *Domain*.Contoso.Com and then select Properties.

9. In the Zone Transfers tab, select Allow Zone Transfers, select To Any Server, and then click OK.

10. Close all open windows.

Verifying Replication and Allowing Zone Transfers

IMPORTANT *Complete this task from the student computer with the lower number. This will ensure that zone transfers are allowed to any server.*

1. Start your computer running Windows Server 2003, and log on as **studentxx@domain.contoso.com** where studentxx is your student User Name and *domain* is the name of your domain.

2. Click Start, click Control Panel, and then double-click Administrative Tools.

3. Right-click DNS, and then select Run As to open the Run As dialog box.

4. In the Run As dialog box, select The Following User option, and then enter the following credentials in the dialog box fields to open the DNS console:

   a. In the User Name box, enter **administrator@*domain*.contoso.com** where *domain* is the name of your domain.

   b. In the Password box, enter **MSPress@LS#1**.

5. Click OK to open the DNS console.

6. In the DNS console tree, expand Computer.*xx* where Computer.*xx* is the name of your computer, expand Forward Lookup Zones, and select *Domain*.Contoso.Com where *Domain*.Contoso.Com is the name of your domain.

7. Right-click *Domain*.Contoso.Com, and then select Properties.

8. In the Zone Transfers tab, ensure that Allow Zone Transfers and To Any Server are selected, and then click OK.

9. Close all open windows.

EXERCISE 4-3: MONITORING AND TROUBLESHOOTING DNS

Estimated completion time: 25 minutes

In this exercise, you will use several tools and utilities to monitor and troubleshoot the DNS Server service. At times, the DNS Server service has support issues that must be fixed. Knowing how to use these tools to support DNS is essential to a network administrator.

Configuring DNS Adapter Settings

> **IMPORTANT**   Complete this task from both student computers. This will allow you to configure the network adapter that is connected to the Contoso Ltd. Network to use your computer's DNS Server service.

1. Start your computer running Windows Server 2003, and log on as **administrator@*domain*.contoso.com** where *domain* is the name of your domain.

2. Click Start, and then click Network Connections to open the Network Connections window.

3. Right-click the Contoso Ltd Network connection icon, and then click Properties.

4. Click Internet Protocol (TCP/IP), and then click Properties.

5. On the Internet Protocol (TCP/IP) Properties page, verify that Use The Following DNS Server Addresses option is selected, then type the IP address of your computer (**10.1.1.*xx***) in the Preferred DNS Server box, and then click OK.

6. Click Close to close the Contoso Ltd Network Properties page.

7. Close all open windows.

Using Dnscmd to Display Records

IMPORTANT *Complete this task from both computers. This will allow you to display information about the zones that are configured and the records that are contained within a DNS zone.*

1. Start your computer running Microsoft Windows Server 2003, and log on as **administrator@*domain*.contoso.com** where *domain* is the name of your domain.

2. Click Start, click All Programs, click Windows Support Tools, and then click Command Prompt.

3. At the C:\Program Files\Support Tools prompt, type **dnscmd /enumzones**, and then press ENTER.

4. In the following chart, list the zones and their individual properties:

Zone Name	Zone Count	Type	Storage	Properties

QUESTION *What is indicated under the Properties heading about the zones?*

5. At the command prompt, type **dnscmd /zoneprint *domain*.contoso.com** where *domain* is the name of your domain, and then press ENTER.

QUESTION *Which types of records are listed in the zone?*

6. Close all open windows.

Using Nslookup to Examine DNS Records

IMPORTANT *Complete this task from both computers. This will allow you to list all resource records in a given domain and zone file.*

1. Start your computer running Microsoft Windows Server 2003, and log on as **administrator@*domain*.contoso.com** where *domain* is the name of your domain.

2. To open a command prompt, click Start, click Run, type **cmd**, and then press ENTER.

3. In the command prompt window, type **nslookup**, and then press ENTER.

4. At the Nslookup prompt, type **set type=all**, and then press ENTER.

5. At the Nslookup prompt, type **ls *domain*.contoso.com** where *domain* is the name of your domain, and then press ENTER.

QUESTION *What would happen if you use the -d option in the ls nslookup command?*

6. Click Start, click Control Panel, click Administrative Tools, and then click DNS.

7. In the DNS console tree, expand Forward Lookup Zones, and expand *Domain*.Contoso.Com where *Domain* is the name of your domain. Use the scope pane to view the resource records in the zone.

8. Use the DNS console to compare the resource records to the results in step 5 using Nslookup.

9. Close all open windows.

Listing DNS Host Records

IMPORTANT   Complete this task from both computers. This will allow you to list host, or A, resource records in a given domain and zone file.

1. Start your computer running Microsoft Windows Server 2003, and then log on as **administrator@*domain*.contoso.com** where *domain* is the name of your domain.

2. To open a command prompt, click Start, click Run, type **cmd**, and then press ENTER.

3. In the command prompt window, type **nslookup**, and then press ENTER.

4. At the Nslookup prompt, type **set type=a**, and then press ENTER.

5. At the Nslookup prompt, type **ls *domain*.contoso.com** where *domain* is the name your domain, and then press ENTER.

6. List the host, or A, records in the following space:

_____

_____

_____

_____

_____

_____

QUESTION   Which NS records did Nslookup return from the query?

QUESTION   What is the NS record used for?

7. Type **exit**, and then press ENTER to exit Nslookup.

8. Close all open windows.

Monitoring the DNS Server Service

IMPORTANT   Complete this task from both student computers. This will allow you to monitor your DNS server.

1. Start your computer running Windows Server 2003, and log on as **student*xx*@*domain*.contoso.com** where student*xx* is your student User Name and *domain* is the name of your domain.

2. Click Start, click Control Panel, and then double-click Administrative Tools.

3. Right-click DNS, and then select Run As to open the Run As dialog box.

4. In the Run As dialog box, select The Following User option, and then enter the following credentials in the dialog box fields to open the DNS console:

   a. In the User Name box, enter **administrator@*domain*.contoso.com** where *domain* is the name of your domain.

   b. In the Password box, enter **MSPress@LS#1**.

5. Click OK to open the DNS console.

6. In the DNS console tree, select and right-click Computer.*xx* where Computer.*xx* is the name of your student computer, and then click Clear Cache from the popup menu.

7. In the DNS console tree, right-click Computer.*xx* where Computer.*xx* is the name of your student computer, and then click Properties.

8. In the properties page, in the Monitoring tab, under Select A Test Type, select both the A Simple Query Against This DNS Server and the A Recursive Query To Other DNS Servers options, and then click Test Now.

   QUESTION   *Why does the recursive query fail when it is tested?*

9. Click OK to close the Computer.*xx* Properties page.

10. In the DNS console tree, right-click Computer.*xx* where Computer.*xx* is the name of your student computer, and then click Clear Cache.

11. In the DNS console tree, right-click Computer.*xx* where Computer.*xx* is the name of your student computer, and then click Properties.

12. In the Forwarders tab, in the Selected Domain's Forwarder IP Address List option, type the IP address of the instructor's machine (10.1.1.200), click Add, and then click OK.

13. Click the Root Hints tab, and in the Name Servers section, select each of the root servers, and then click Remove.

14. In the Root Hints tab, click Add. In the New Resource Record page, in the Server Fully Qualified Domain Name (FQDN) field, type **instructor01.contoso.com**. In the IP address field, type **10.1.1.200**, click Add, and then click OK.

15. On the Computer.*xx* Properties page, click Apply.

16. In the Monitoring tab, under Select A Test Type, ensure that both the A Simple Query Against This DNS Server and the A Recursive Query To Other DNS Servers options are selected, and then click Test Now.

   QUESTION   *Why does the recursive query pass when it is tested this time?*

17. In the Forwarders tab, in the Selected Domain's Forwarder IP Address List option, click Remove, and then click OK.

18. Close all open windows.

EXERCISE 4-4: MANAGING DNS

Estimated completion time: 15 minutes

In this exercise, you will use several tools to manage your DNS server.

The Ipconfig Utility

IMPORTANT   Complete this task from both computers. This will allow you to display the pertinent DNS-related switches when using the Ipconfig utility.

1. Start your computer running Windows Server 2003, and log on as **administrator@*domain*.contoso.com** where *domain* is the name of your domain.

2. To open a command prompt, click Start, click Run, type **cmd**, and then press ENTER.

3. At the command prompt, type **ipconfig /?**, and then press ENTER.

   QUESTION   Which Ipconfig switches relate to DNS? Name them and explain each of their functions.

4. Close the command prompt window.

Preloading the DNS Resolver Cache

IMPORTANT   Complete this task from both computers. This will allow you to preload the DNS resolver cache on your student computer.

1. Start your computer running Microsoft Windows Server 2003, and log on as **administrator@*domain*.contoso.com** where *domain* is the name of your domain.

2. To open a command prompt, click Start, click Run, and then type **cmd**.

3. At the command prompt, type **ipconfig /displaydns**.

   QUESTION   Why are there entries listed?

4. At the command prompt, type **ipconfig /flushdns**, and then press ENTER.

5. Click Start, and then click My Computer to open the contents of My Computer.

6. Locate the following file: %systemroot%\System32\Drivers\Etc\Hosts.

7. Right-click the Hosts file, select Open, and in the Open With window, double-click Notepad.

8. In the line # 102.54.94.97 rhino.acme.com, remove the pound (#) sign from the beginning of the line.

9. Click File, and then click Save.

10. Close Microsoft Notepad and the C:\%systemroot%\system32\drivers\etc window.

11. In the command prompt window, type **ipconfig /displaydns**.

   QUESTION   Is there an entry for rhino.acme.com? How was this loaded into the DNS resolver cache?

Configuring DNS Scavenging

IMPORTANT   Complete this task from both computers. This will allow you to set scavenging for a specific DNS zone.

1. Start your computer running Windows Server 2003, and log on as **studentxx@domain.contoso.com** where student*xx* is your student User Name and *domain* is the name of your domain.

2. Click Start, click Control Panel, and then click Administrative Tools.

3. Right-click DNS, and then select Run As to open the Run As dialog box.

4. In the Run As dialog box, select The Following User option, and then enter the following credentials in the dialog box fields to open the DNS console:

   a. In the User Name box, enter **administrator@domain.contoso.com** where *domain* is the name of your domain.

   b. In the Password box, enter **MSPress@LS#1**.

5. Click OK to open the DNS console.

6. In the DNS console tree, expand Computer*xx* where Computer*xx* is the name of your student computer, and then expand Forward Lookup Zones.

7. In the DNS console tree, select and right-click the *Domain*.Contoso.Com where *domain* is the name of your domain, and then click Properties.

8. On the *Domain*.Contoso.Com Properties page, click the General tab, and then click Aging to open the Zone Aging/Scavenging Properties window.

9. Select the Scavenge Stale Resource Records option, and then click OK.

10. Click OK.

   QUESTION   What does it mean to scavenge stale resource records?

11. Close all open windows.

Enabling WINS Lookup

IMPORTANT   Complete this task from both computers. This will allow you to enable Windows Internet Naming Service (WINS) lookup for DNS.

1. Start your computer running Windows Server 2003, and log on as **studentxx@domain.contoso.com** where student*xx* is your student User Name and *domain* is the name of your domain.

2. Click Start, click Control Panel, and then double-click Administrative Tools.

3. Right-click DNS, and then select click Run As to open the Run As dialog box.

4. In the Run As dialog box, select The Following User option, and enter the following credentials in the dialog box fields to open the DNS console:

    a. In the User Name box, enter **administrator@*domain*.contoso.com** where *domain* is the name of your domain.

    b. In the Password box, enter **MSPress@LS#1**.

5. Click OK to open the DNS console.

6. In the DNS console tree, expand Computer.*xx* where Computer.*xx* is the name of your student computer, and then expand Forward Lookup Zones.

7. Select and right-click *Domain*.Contoso.Com where *domain* is the name of your domain, and then click Properties.

8. On the *Domain*.Contoso.Com Properties page, click the WINS tab, select the Use WINS Forward Lookup option, and then enter your computer's IP address in the IP Address section. Click Add, and then click OK.

QUESTION   After enabling WINS lookup, which resource record is added to the DNS zone in the DNS console?

9. Close all open windows.

EXERCISE 4-5: SECURING DNS

Estimated completion time: 10 minutes

In this exercise, you will use several methods to secure DNS. It is essential to secure DNS to guard against unauthorized access.

Security on the DNS Server

IMPORTANT   Complete this task from both computers. This will allow you to review the security settings for which users and groups currently have access to manage and monitor the DNS server.

1. Start your computer running Windows Server 2003, and log on as **student*xx*@*domain*.contoso.com** where student.*xx* is your student User Name and *domain* is the name of your domain.

2. Click Start, click Control Panel, and then double-click Administrative Tools.

3. Right-click DNS, and select Run As to open the Run As dialog box.

4. In the Run As dialog box, select The Following User option, and enter the following credentials in the dialog box fields to open the DNS console:

    a. In the User Name box, enter **administrator@*domain*.contoso.com** where *domain* is the name of your domain.

    b. In the Password box, enter **MSPress@LS#1**.

5. Click OK to open the DNS console.

6. In the DNS console tree, select and right-click Computer*xx* where Computer*xx* is the name of your student computer, and then click Properties.

7. Click the Security tab to display the discretionary access control list (DACL) for the DNS server.

   QUESTION   Why isn't the Everyone group listed in the DACL?

8. Click OK, and then close all open windows.

Security on the DNS Zone

IMPORTANT   Complete this task from both computers. This will allow you to review the security settings for the DNS zone.

1. Start your computer running Windows Server 2003, and log on as **student*xx*@*domain*.contoso.com** where student*xx* is your student User Name and *domain* is the name of your domain.

2. Click Start, click Control Panel, and then double-click Administrative Tools.

3. Right-click DNS, and then select Run As to open the Run As dialog box.

4. In the Run As dialog box, select The Following User option, and then enter the following credentials in the dialog box fields to open the DNS console:

   a. In the User Name box, enter **administrator@*domain*.contoso.com** where *domain* is the name of your domain.

   b. In the Password box, enter **MSPress@LS#1**.

5. Click OK to open the DNS console.

6. In the DNS console tree, expand Computer*xx* where Computer*xx* is the name of your student computer, and then expand Forward Lookup Zones.

7. In the DNS console tree, select and right-click *Domain*.Contoso.Com, and then click Properties.

8. On the *Domain*.Contoso.Com Properties page, click the Security tab to display the DACL for the DNS zone.

   QUESTION   Why is the Everyone group listed in the DACL?

9. Click OK, and then close all open windows.

Configuring a Listener

IMPORTANT   Complete this task from both computers. This will allow you to configure a listener for the DNS Server service.

1. Start your computer running Windows Server 2003, and log on as **student*xx*@*domain*.contoso.com** where student*xx* is your student User Name and *domain* is the name of your domain.

2. Click Start, click Control Panel, and then click Administrative Tools.

3. Right-click DNS, and then select Run As to open the Run As dialog box.

4. In the Run As dialog box, select The Following User option, and then enter the following credentials in the dialog box fields to open the DNS console:

   a. In the User Name field, enter **administrator@ *domain*.contoso.com** where *domain* is the name of your domain.

   b. In the Password field, enter **MSPress@LS#1**.

5. Click OK to open the DNS console.

6. In the DNS console tree, select and right-click Computer*xx* where Computer*xx* is the name of your student computer, and then click Properties.

7. On the Computer*xx* Properties page, in the Interfaces tab, select Only The Following IP Addresses. Verify that your Contoso network adapter IP address (10.1.1.*xx*) is listed in the IP Address list, and then click OK.

   QUESTION   How does configuring a listener secure the DNS server?

8. Close all open windows.

Securing Zone Transfers

IMPORTANT   Complete this task from both computers. This will allow you to secure DNS zone transfers for the DNS server.

1. Start your computer running Windows Server 2003, and log on as **student*xx*@*domain*.contoso.com** where student*xx* is your student User Name and *domain* is the name of your domain.

2. Click Start, click Control Panel, and then double-click Administrative Tools.

3. Right-click DNS, and then select Run As to open the Run As dialog box.

4. In the Run As dialog box, select The Following User option, and then enter the following credentials in the dialog box fields to open the DNS console:

   a. In the User Name box, enter **administrator@*domain*.contoso.com** where *domain* is the name of your domain.

   b. In the Password box, enter **MSPress@LS#1**.

5. Click OK to open the DNS console.

6. In the DNS console tree, expand Computer*xx* where Computer*xx* is the name of your student computer, and then expand Forward Lookup Zones.

7. Select and right-click *Domain*.Contoso.Com where *Domain* is the name of your domain, and then click Properties.

8. On the *Domain*.Contoso.Com Properties page, in the Zone Transfers tab, ensure that Allow Zone Transfers is selected, and that the Only To The Following Servers is selected.

9. In the IP Address section, type the IP address of the instructor's computer **(10.1.1.200)**, and then click Add.

10. Click OK.

   QUESTION   *How does configuring zone transfers secure the DNS server?*

11. Close all open windows.

EXERCISE 4-6: REMOVING THE DNS SERVER SERVICE

Estimated completion time: 5 minutes

You will now remove the DNS Server service from your student computers. This is necessary for the successful completion of future labs.

Removing the DNS Server Service

IMPORTANT   *Complete this task from both student computers. This will allow you to remove the DNS Server service from your student computer.*

1. Start your computer running Windows Server 2003, and log on as **student*xx*@*domain*.contoso.com** where student*xx* is your student User Name and *domain* is the name of your domain.

2. Click Start, click Control Panel, and then double-click Administrative Tools.

3. Right-click the Manage Your Server option, and then click Run As to open the Run As dialog box.

4. Select The Following User option, and then enter the following credentials in the dialog box fields to open the Manage Your Server wizard:

   a. In the User Name box, enter **administrator@*domain*.contoso.com** where *domain* is the name of your domain.

   b. In the Password box, enter **MSPress@LS#1**.

5. Click OK to open Manage Your Server.

6. In Manage Your Server, click Add Or Remove A Role to open the Configure Your Server wizard.

7. On the Preliminary Steps page of the Configure Your Server wizard, click Next.

8. On the Server Role page, select DNS Server, and then click Next.

9. On the Role Removal Confirmation page, click Remove The DNS Server Role option, and then click Next.

10. On the DNS Server Role Removed page, click Finish.

11. Close all open windows.

Configuring DNS Adapter Settings

IMPORTANT *Complete this task from both student computers. This will allow you to configure the network adapter, which is connected to the Contoso Ltd. Network with a DNS server IP address. Your server therefore becomes a DNS client of the DNS Server service that runs on the instructor's computer.*

1. Start your computer running Windows Server 2003, and log on as **administrator@*domain*.contoso.com** where *domain* is the name of your domain.

2. Click Start, and then click Network Connections to open the Network Connections window.

3. Right-click the Contoso Ltd Network connection icon, and then click Properties.

4. Click Internet Protocol (TCP/IP), and then click Properties.

5. On the Internet Protocol (TCP/IP) Properties page, verify that Use The Following DNS Server Addresses is selected, type your instructor's computer's IP address (**10.1.1.200**) in the Preferred DNS Server box, and then click OK.

6. Click Close to close the Contoso Ltd Network Properties page.

7. Close all open windows.

LAB REVIEW QUESTIONS

Estimated completion time: 15 minutes

1. Which three methods presented in this Lab can you use to secure a DNS server and zone data?

2. Which file is used to preload the DNS resolver cache?

3. Which utility can be used to view DNS events that are recorded?

4. Which two utilities presented earlier in this Lab can be helpful in managing and troubleshooting DNS problems?

5. When are updates to an Active Directory–integrated zone file replicated?

6. What is the difference between a simple (iterative) and a recursive query?

7. Name a tool other than Active Directory Sites And Services that is covered in the labs and that can be used to force replication of Active Directory–integrated zones.

LAB CHALLENGE 4-1: INSTALLING AND MANAGING DNS

Estimated completion time: 30 minutes

You have been hired as a network consultant for Northwind Traders to help the company configure and monitor the DNS servers on its network. The Information Services (IS) department for Northwind Traders has deployed several Active

Directory domain controllers that reside within two domains: nwtraders.com and europe.nwtraders.com. A DNS server in the nwtraders.com domain runs a standard primary zone called nwtraders.com. Two DNS servers are in the europe.nwtraders.com child domain: the first DNS server runs a standard primary zone, and the second DNS server runs a standard secondary zone. Each local area network (LAN) also contains multiple DHCP servers and WINS servers. Client computers on the LANs use DHCP for IP addressing.

As the consultant, you have been asked to help resolve DNS-related issues for the IS department. The department would like to configure the DNS infrastructure to lessen the administrative effort associated with managing the DNS servers and DNS zone files and to reduce internal network traffic. IS personnel have also asked you to assist them in securing the DNS servers and zone transfers within the network and in verifying, testing, and monitoring DNS activity. And last, to save on wide area network (WAN) link bandwidth, the IS department wants to be able to configure the DNS servers to forward DNS queries to internal DNS servers, rather than having all DNS servers forwarding DNS queries to the Internet.

TROUBLESHOOTING LAB
DEPLOYING NETWORK SERVICES

REVIEWING THE PROJECT

You are a member of a team of network engineers for Contoso, Ltd. You are in charge of planning and implementing a network services strategy for the company network. Your job is to plan and implement a Dynamic Host Configuration Protocol (DHCP) Internet Protocol (IP) addressing strategy and a Domain Name System (DNS) name resolution strategy for your network. Implementing these two network services will allow you to communicate with client and server computers using host names and IP addresses. The Contoso network consists of one domain, contoso.com, and several child domains. The clients and servers on the network must also be capable of resolving internal child domain host names.

Currently, the clients and servers on the network are all configured to use static IP addressing, which includes the IP address for a DNS server. You also must limit bandwidth that is utilized by these network services and client computers in the internal child domain.

Based on what you know about the Contoso network infrastructure, and keeping in mind that you must limit network traffic, answer each of the following questions. Include an explanation with each answer.

1. How many DHCP servers will you need to configure for the Contoso network?

2. How many DNS servers will you need to configure for the Contoso network?

3. At a minimum, which DHCP options should you assign?

4. Should you configure a DHCP relay agent on each of the subnets to allow DHCP clients to obtain IP addressing information from a remote DHCP server?

To experiment with DHCP and DNS within a networked environment, you want to configure a test network that will be used to install and configure DHCP and DNS. This test network will be configured with an IP subnet of 192.168.0.0/24. This test environment will consist of one student computer acting as a server computer and one student computer acting as a client computer.

Your deployment should include the following tasks:

■ Install and deploy a DHCP server on a Microsoft Windows Server 2003 computer.

73

- Configure a DHCP server to respond to IP address lease requests.
- Configure a DHCP server to give out the appropriate IP addressing scope options.
- Install and deploy a DNS server infrastructure on a computer that runs Windows Server 2003.

When you are finished, be prepared to demonstrate to your instructor that your servers can:

- Communicate using Transmission Control Protocol/Ineternet Protocol (TCP/IP).
- Receive dynamic IP Adressesing information through DHCP.
- Communicate using the DNS Server service to resolve internal child domain host names.

TROUBLESHOOTING SETUP

In this part of the troubleshooting lab, your instructor or fellow students will introduce a malfunction into your network that will prevent network IP address assignment and name resolution from occurring.

TROUBLESHOOTING

In this portion of the troubleshooting lab, you are assigned to resolve a communication problem introduced in the previous section of the lab. As you proceed with the troubleshooting process, documenting the processes you use to fix the problem is crucial to your overall success. Record the steps and troubleshooting processes, and include information such as the following:

- What did you look at to diagnose the problem? List the steps you took to diagnose the problem, even the ones that didn't work.
- What was the problem you discovered? What was the cause of the problem?
- What was the solution? What steps did you take to resolve the problem?
- What tests did you perform to confirm the problem's resolution, and what are the results of these tests?
- List the resources you used to help solve the problem.

The malfunctions introduced on the networks are designed to inhibit communications in some way—either between the computers in the child domain, or between domain computers and the other domains in the classroom. You can use the Ping utility, Tracert utility, Nslookup utility, Dnscmd utility, or any other utilities to test the connections and help troubleshoot the problem.

LAB 5
NETWORK SECURITY

This lab contains the following exercises and activities:

- Exercise 5-1: Auditing Security

- Exercise 5-2: Applying Security Templates

- Exercise 5-3: Assigning User Rights

- Exercise 5-4: Using Encrypting File System (EFS)

- Exercise 5-5: Installing and Configuring Microsoft Baseline Security Analyzer (MBSA)

- Lab Review Questions

- Lab Challenge 5-1: Wingtip Toys Security Plan

After completing this lab, you will be able to

- Audit security events on a domain controller.

- Analyze and apply security settings to a server computer.

- Encrypt and decrypt files stored locally and remotely.

- Use MBSA to scan and detect security vulnerabilities.

Estimated completion time: 115 minutes

SCENARIO

You are the network administrator for Northwind Traders. You have been asked to recommend several security practices to increase the level of security for the network. You will be in charge of hardening servers and domain controllers and running Microsoft Baseline Security Analyzer (MBSA) to detect security vulnerabilities on workstations and servers on the network.

To ensure the security of data both locally and remotely, you must encrypt files using Encrypting File System (EFS) for clients and servers on the network. You also must designate a recovery agent for the domain.

EXERCISE 5-1: AUDITING SECURITY

Estimated completion time: 5 minutes

In this exercise, you will learn how to configure security auditing, and you will review security auditing on a server running Microsoft Windows Server 2003.

Auditing Security Events

IMPORTANT   *Complete this task from both student computers. This will allow you to view security auditing on a domain controller.*

1. Start your computer running Windows Server 2003, and log on as **student*xx*@*domain*.contoso.com** (where student*xx* is your student User Name and *domain* is the name of your domain).

2. Click Start, select Control Panel, and then double-click Administrative Tools.

3. Right-click Event Viewer, and then select Run As to open the Run As dialog box.

4. In the Run As dialog box, select The Following User option, and then enter the following credentials in the dialog box fields to open the Event Viewer console:

    a. In the User Name box, enter **administrator@*domain*.contoso.com** (where *domain* is the name of your domain).

    b. In the Password box, enter **MSPress@LS#1**.

5. Click OK to open the Event Viewer console.

6. In the console tree, click Security in the scope pane.

    QUESTION   *Name three categories of events that are recorded in the security log on your server.*

7. Minimize the Event Viewer window.

8. Click Start, select Control Panel, and then double-click Administrative Tools.

9. Right-click Domain Controller Security Policy, and then select Run As to open the Run As dialog box.

10. In the Run As dialog box, select The Following User option, and then enter the following credentials in the dialog box fields to open the Domain Controller Security Policy console:

    a. In the User Name box, enter **administrator@*domain*.contoso.com** (where *domain* is the name of your domain).

    b. In the Password box, enter **MSPress@LS#1**.

11. Click OK to open the Domain Controller Security Policy console.

12. Expand Local Policies, and then click Audit Policy.

13. In the details pane, double-click Audit Object Access.

14. In the Audit Object Access Properties window, click the Success option, and then click OK.

15. Close the Domain Controller Security Policy console.

16. Right-click your desktop, select New, and then select Folder.

17. Type **computer.xx** as the name of the folder (where computer.xx is the name of your student computer).

18. Right click on the folder computerxx and choose Properties.

19. On the computerxx Properties page, click the Security tab and then click on the Advanced button.

20. On the Advanced Security Settings for computerxx, click on the Auditing tab and click Add.

21. On Select User, Computer, or Group screen, click Advanced and click Find Now.

22. In the drop down display, double click on the Users group and click OK.

23. On the Auditing Entry for computerxx, check the Successful box for List Folder/Read Data and click OK.

24. Click OK to close the Advanced Security Settings for computerxx.

25. Click OK to close the computerxx Properties page.

26. Double-click the folder you just created on the desktop.

27. Close the computerxx folder.

28. Maximize Event Viewer, and then press F5.

In the details pane, notice that events of the category Object Access were written to the security log.

29. Double click on the Object Access Events and verify that there is an event related to accessing the computerxx folder in step 26.

30. Close Event Viewer.

EXERCISE 5-2: APPLYING SECURITY TEMPLATES

Estimated completion time: 15 minutes

In this exercise, you will learn how to use the Security Configuration And Analysis Microsoft Management Console (MMC) snap-in to compare security settings on your student computer. You will also learn how to use the Gpupdate tool to apply defined security templates to your computer. You will then reapply the Setup Security template to bring your system back to the state it was in when it was installed.

Creating a Security Settings Console

IMPORTANT   *Complete this task from both student computers. This will allow you to create a new MMC containing the Security Templates snap-in and the Security Configuration And Analysis snap-in.*

1. Start your computer running Windows Server 2003, and log on as **administrator@***domain***.contoso.com** (where *domain* is the name of your domain).
2. Click Start, and then click Run to open the Run dialog box.
3. In the Open box, type **mmc**, and then click OK.
4. In the Console1 window, on the File menu, select Add/Remove Snap-In to open the Add/Remove Snap-In dialog box.
5. Click Add.
6. Scroll down the list of available snap-ins, select Security Configuration And Analysis, and then click Add.
7. Select Security Templates, and then click Add.
8. Click Close to close the Add Stand Alone Snap-In window, and then click OK.
9. On the File menu, select Save As.
10. In the Save As window, click the desktop icon, and then in the File Name box, type **security**. Click Save.
11. Close all open windows.

Comparing Security Settings Using the Security Configuration And Analysis MMC Snap-In

IMPORTANT   *Complete this task from both student computers. This will allow you to compare security settings on your student computer to predefined security templates.*

1. Start your computer running Windows Server 2003, and log on as **administrator@***domain***.contoso.com** (where *domain* is the name of your domain).
2. Double-click the security MMC icon on the desktop to open the MMC.
3. Select Security Configuration And Analysis in the console tree.
4. On the Action menu, select Open Database to open the Open Database window.
5. In the File Name box, type **securedc**, and then click Open.
6. In the Import Template window, click Securedc.inf, and then click Open.
7. Select Security Configuration And Analysis in the console tree if it is not already selected.
8. On the Action menu, select Analyze Computer Now.
9. Accept the default error log path in the Perform Analysis window, and then click OK.

10. In the console tree, expand Security Configuration And Analysis\Local Policies, and then select Audit Policy.

11. In the details pane, locate Audit Account Logon Events.

    Record the settings below:

Database Setting	Computer Setting

12. Leave the console open.

    QUESTION   Why is there a red X on the Audit Logon Events policy?

    QUESTION   Why would you want to record the successes and failures of logon events?

Applying Security Templates

IMPORTANT   Complete this task from both student computers. This will allow you to apply a predefined security template to your student computer.

1. Select Security Configuration And Analysis in the console tree.

2. On the Action menu, select Configure Computer Now.

3. Accept the default error log path in the Configure System window, and then click OK.

4. Leave the console open.

Verifying Imported Security Settings Using the Security Configuration And Analysis MMC Snap-In

IMPORTANT   Complete this task from both student computers. This will allow you to compare security settings on your student computer to predefined security templates.

1. Select Security Configuration And Analysis in the console tree.

2. On the Action menu, select Analyze Computer Now.

3. Click OK to accept the default error log path.

4. In the console tree, expand Security Configuration And Analysis\Local Policies, and then select Audit Policy.

5. In the details pane, locate Audit Logon Events.

    Record the settings below:

Database Setting	Computer Setting

6. Leave the Security console open.

    QUESTION   Why is there a green check mark on Audit Logon Events?

Reapplying the Setup Security Template Settings

IMPORTANT   *Complete this task from both student computers. This will allow you to reapply the Setup Security template to bring your security settings on your student computer back to the initial state.*

1. Select Security Configuration And Analysis in the console tree.
2. On the Action menu, select Open Database to open the Open Database window.
3. In the File Name box, type **setup security**, and then click Open.
4. In the Import Template window, click Setup Security.inf, and then click Open.
5. On the Action menu, select Configure Computer Now.
6. Accept the default error log path on the Configure System window, and then click OK.
7. Close the Security console.

EXERCISE 5-3: ASSIGNING USER RIGHTS

Estimated completion time: 5 minutes

In this exercise, you will learn how to configure and assign user rights to a computer running Windows Server 2003.

Assigning the Logon Locally Right

IMPORTANT   *Complete this task from both student computers. This will allow you to configure user rights to allow a new student account to log on locally to your student computer.*

1. Start your computer running Windows Server 2003, and log on as **administrator@*domain*.contoso.com** (where *domain* is the name of your domain).
2. Click Start, click Administrative Tools, and then click Active Directory Users And Computers.
3. In the Active Directory Users And Computers console tree, select the Students organizational unit (OU).
4. In the Active Directory Users And Computers console tree, right-click the Students OU, click New, and then click User to open the New Object— User window.
5. In the New Object—User window, in the First name box, type **studentlogon**.
6. In the New Object—User window, in the User Logon Name box, type **studentlogon**, and then click Next.
7. In the Password and Confirm Password fields, type **studentlogon**, clear the User Must Change Password At Next Logon option, click the User Cannot Change Password option, and then click Next.

8. In the New Object—User window, click Finish to finish creating the new user account.

9. Close the Active Directory Users And Computers console.

10. Click Start, click Administrative Tools, and then click Domain Controller Security Policy.

11. Under the Security Setting node, expand Local Policies.

12. Select User Rights Assignment, and in the details pane, double-click Allow Log On Locally.

13. On the Allow Log On Locally Properties page, click Add User Or Group.

14. In the Add User Or Group window, click Browse.

15. Click the Advanced button in the Select Users, Computers, Or Groups window.

16. Click Find Now.

17. Select the studentlogon account in the search results pane, and then click OK.

18. Click OK in the Select Users, Computers, Or Groups window.

19. Click OK in the Add User Or Groups dialog box.

20. Click OK to close the Allow Logon Locally Properties window.

21. Close the Domain Controller Security Policy console window.

EXERCISE 5-4: USING ENCRYPTING FILE SYSTEM (EFS)

Estimated completion time: 50 minutes

In this exercise, you will encrypt and decrypt folders using Windows Explorer and using the command-line utility Cipher. You will also learn how to implement EFS in different situations, and you will learn how to assign a designated recovery agent for a domain.

Encrypting and Decrypting Files and Folders

IMPORTANT Complete this task from both student computers. This will allow you to encrypt and decrypt files and folders using Windows Explorer.

1. Start your computer running Windows Server 2003, and log on as **studentxx@domain.contoso.com** (where studentxx is your student User Name and *domain* is the name of your domain).

2. Right-click on your desktop, click New, and then select Folder.

3. Type **encrypted folder** as the name of the folder.

4. Double-click Encrypted Folder, which you just created on the desktop.

5. In the Encrypted Folder window, click File, click New, and then click Text Document.

6. Type **encrypted file** as the name of the file, and then press ENTER.

7. Right-click Encrypted File, and then select Properties.

8. In the General tab, click Advanced to open the Advanced Attributes window.

9. In the Advanced Attributes window, click the Encrypt Contents To Secure Data option, and then click OK.

10. Click OK to close the Encrypted File Properties window.

11. In the Encryption Warning window, select Encrypt The File Only, and then click OK.

12. Notice that the text labeling the encrypted file turns green, indicating the file has been encrypted.

   QUESTION   How can you change whether a different colored label is used to indicate that a file is encrypted?

13. Close the Encrypted Folder window.

Using Cipher to Encrypt and Decrypt Folders

   IMPORTANT   Complete this task from both student computers. This will allow you to encrypt and decrypt files and folders using the Cipher utility.

1. Start your computer running Windows Server 2003, and log on as **student*xx*@*domain*.contoso.com** (where student*xx* is your student User Name and *domain* is the name of your domain).

2. Double-click Encrypted Folder that was created on the desktop.

3. In the Encrypted Folder window, click File, click New, and then click Text Document.

4. Type **ciphertext-unencrypted** as the name of the file, and then leave the folder open.

5. Click Start, and then click Run to open the Run dialog box.

6. In the Open box, type **cmd**, and then click OK to open the Cmd.exe window.

7. At the command prompt, type **cd desktop** to change the command prompt path.

8. At the command prompt, type **cd encrypted folder** to change the command prompt path.

9. At the command prompt, type **cipher**.

   Record the results below:

Attribute	File Name

   QUESTION   What does the attribute tell you about the encryption state of the files?

10. In the Encrypted Folder window, click File, click New, click Folder, and then type **encrypted-subfolder**.

11. At the command prompt, type **cipher /e /s:encrypted-subfolder**.

12. At the command prompt, type **cipher**.

Record the results below:

Attribute	File Name

13. At the command prompt, type **cipher /d /s:encrypted-subfolder**.

14. At the command prompt, type **cipher**.

Record the results below:

Attribute	File Name

15. Close all open windows.

Increasing the Domain Functional Level

IMPORTANT *Complete this task from the student computer with the lower number. This will allow you to increase the domain functional level for your domain.*

1. Start your computer running Windows Server 2003, and log on as **studentxx@domain.contoso.com** (where studentxx is your student User Name and *domain* is the name of your domain).

2. Click Start, select Control Panel, and then double-click Administrative Tools.

3. Right-click Active Directory Users And Computers, and then select Run As to open the Run As dialog box.

4. In the Run As dialog box, select The Following User option, and then enter the following credentials in the dialog box fields to open the Active Directory Users And Computers console:

   a. In the User Name box, enter **administrator@domain.contoso.com** (where *domain* is the name of your domain).

   b. In the Password box, enter **MSPress@LS#1**.

5. Click OK to open the Active Directory Users And Computers console.

6. In the console tree, select and right-click *Domain*.Contoso.Com (where *Domain* is the name of your domain), and then click Raise Domain Functional Level to open the Raise Domain Functional Level window.

7. Select Windows Server 2003 from the Select An Available Domain Functional Level option.

8. Click the Raise button to raise the domain functional level.

9. Click OK in the Raise Domain Functional Level Warning dialog box.

10. Click OK in the Raise Domain Functional Level information box.

Enabling Remote Encryption

IMPORTANT   *Complete this task from the student computer with the lower number. This will allow you to encrypt and decrypt files and folders using remote encryption.*

1. Start your computer running Windows Server 2003, and log on as **student*xx*@domain.contoso.com** (where student*xx* is your student User Name and *domain* is the name of your domain).

2. Click Start, select Control Panel, and then double-click Administrative Tools.

3. Right-click Active Directory Users And Computers, and then select Run As to open the Run As dialog box.

4. Select The Following User option, and then enter the following credentials in the dialog box fields:

   a. In the User Name box, enter **administrator@*domain*.contoso.com** (where *domain* is the name of your domain)

   b. In the Password box, enter **MSPress@LS#1**.

5. Click OK to open the Active Directory Users And Computers console.

6. In the console tree, expand *Domain*.Contoso.Com (where *Domain* is the name of your domain).

7. Select Domain Controller in the console tree.

8. In the details pane, right-click Computer*xx* (where Computer*xx* is the name of your student computer), and then click Properties to open the Computer*xx* Properties window.

9. In the Delegation tab, verify that Trust This Computer For Delegation To Any Service (Kerberos Only) is selected.

10. Click OK to close the Computer*xx* Properties window.

IMPORTANT   *Complete the following tasks from the student computer with the lower number.*

1. Start your computer running Windows Server 2003, and log on as **administrator@*domain*.contoso.com** (where *domain* is the name of your domain).

2. Right-click your desktop, click New, and then select Folder.

3. Type **remote encryption** as the name of the folder.

4. Right-click the Remote Encryption folder, and then select Properties.

5. Click the Sharing tab, and then select the Share This Folder option.

6. Type **remote encryption** in the Share Name box to share the folder.

7. Click the Permissions button to open the Permissions For Remote Encryption window.

8. Select the Allow On Full Control check box in the Permissions For Everyone section.

9. Click OK to accept your permission changes.

10. Click the Security tab.

11. Click Add under Group Or User Names, and then click Advanced.

12. Click Find Now in the Select Users, Computers, Or Groups window.

13. Choose the Everyone Group from the drop-down list, and then click OK.

14. Click OK again to close the Select Users, Computers, Or Groups window.

15. In the Remote Encryption Properties window, select Everyone, select the Full Control option under Permissions For Everyone, and then click OK to close the properties page.

IMPORTANT Complete the following tasks from the student computer with the higher number.

1. Start your computer running Windows Server 2003, and log on as **student*xx*@*domain*.contoso.com** (where student*xx* is your student User Name and *domain* is the name of your domain).

2. Click Start, and then select Run to open the Run window.

3. In the Open box, type **\\10.1.1.*xx*\remote encryption** (where 10.1.1.*xx* is the IP address of the lower-numbered computer).

4. In the Remote Folder on computer*xx*, click File, click New, and then click Text Document.

5. Type **remotely encrypted.txt** as the name of the file.

6. Right-click the Remotely Encrypted file, and then select Properties.

7. In the General tab, click the Advanced button to open the Advanced Attributes window.

8. In the Advanced Attributes window, click the Encrypt Contents To Secure Data option, and then click OK.

9. Click OK to close the Remotely Encrypted.txt Properties window.

10. Notice that the black label of the Remotely Encrypted file turns green, which indicates that it has been encrypted.

11. Close the Remote Folder window.

Configuring a Data Recovery Agent for an OU

IMPORTANT Complete this task from both student computers. This will allow you to assign a data recovery agent for the Students OU.

1. Start your computer running Windows Server 2003, and log on as **administrator@*domain*.contoso.com** (where *domain* is the name of your domain).

2. Click Start, click Administrative Tools, and then click Active Directory Users And Computers.

3. In the console tree, select *Domain*.Contoso.Com (where *domain* is the name of your domain).

4. In the details pane, right-click Students, and then select Properties to open the Students Properties window.

5. Click the Group Policy tab to open the Current Group Policy Links For Students page.

6. Click New, type **data recovery agent**, and then press ENTER.

7. Click Edit to open the Group Policy Object Editor window.

8. In the Group Policy Object Editor window, expand Computer Configuration \Windows Settings\Security Settings\Public Key Policies, and then select Encrypting File System.

   QUESTION   Are there any EFS policies defined in the details pane?

9. Leave the Active Directory Users And Computers console open.

10. Click Start, and then click Run to open the Run dialog box.

11. In the Open box, type **mmc**, and then click OK to open the Console1 window.

12. On the File menu, select Add/Remove Snap-In to open the Add/Remove Snap-In dialog box.

13. Click Add.

14. Scroll down the list of available snap-ins, select Certificates, and then click Add.

15. In the Certificates snap-in window, select the My User Account option, and then click Finish.

16. Click Close to close the Add Standalone Snap-In window, and then click OK.

17. On the File menu, select Save As.

18. In the Save As window, click the desktop icon, and in the filename box, type **certificates**, and then click Save.

19. Leave the console open.

Exporting a Data Recovery Agent Certificate

IMPORTANT   Complete this task from both student computers. This will allow you to assign a data recovery agent for the Students OU.

1. In the Certificates console, expand Certificates-Current User\Personal, and then select Certificates.

2. In the details pane, locate Administrator in the Issued To column, and then locate File Recovery in the Intended Purposes column.

3. Right-click this certificate, click All Tasks, and then click Export to open the Certificate Export Wizard page.

4. On the Certificate Export Wizard page, click Next.

5. Verify that the No, Do Not Export The Private Key option is selected, and then click Next.

6. Verify that the DER Encoded Binary X.509 (.CER) option is selected, and then click Next.

7. Click the Browse button to open the Save As window.

8. Click the desktop icon in the Save As window, and in the File Name box, type **data recovery certificate**, and then click Save.

9. On the File To Export page, click Next.

10. Click Finish on the Completing The Certificate Export Wizard page.

11. In the dialog box stating that the export was successful, click OK.

Assigning a Data Recovery Agent for an OU

IMPORTANT   *Complete this task from both student computers. This will allow you to assign a data recovery agent for the Students OU.*

1. In the Group Policy Object Editor window for the Students OU, expand Computer Configuration\Windows Settings\Security Settings\Public Key Policies, and then select Encrypting File System.

2. Right-click Encrypting File System, and then select the Add Data Recovery Agent to open the Add Recovery Agent Wizard page.

3. On the Welcome To The Add Recovery Agent Wizard page, click Next to open the Select Recovery Agents page.

4. On the Select Recovery Agents page, click the Browse Folders button.

5. Click the desktop icon on the left, click the Data Recovery Certificate.cer file, and then click Open.

6. In the Add Recovery Agent window, click Yes to install the certificate.

7. On the Select Recovery Agents page, click Next.

8. On the Completing The Add Recovery Agent Wizard page, click Finish.

9. Close all open windows.

EXERCISE 5-5: INSTALLING AND CONFIGURING MICROSOFT BASELINE SECURITY ANALYZER (MBSA)

Estimated completion time: 10 minutes

IMPORTANT   *To complete this exercise, you must download MBSA from the instructor's shared network folder. (Go to http://www.microsoft.com/downloads and search on Microsoft Baseline Security Analyzer for additional information about this tool.)*

In this exercise, you will learn how to install and configure MBSA and Mbsacli. You will then use both interfaces to scan your computer for security vulnerabilities.

Installing MBSA

IMPORTANT *Complete this task from both student computers. This will allow you to install MBSA on your student computer.*

1. Start your computer running Windows Server 2003, and log on as **administrator@***domain***.contoso.com** (where *domain* is the name of your domain).

2. Double-click the Mbsasetup.msi file to open the Microsoft Baseline Security Analyzer Setup Wizard.

3. On the Welcome page, click Next.

4. On the License Agreement page, review the license agreement, and then click Accept The License Agreement if you agree with the terms. (If you do not agree with the terms, you cannot continue with this installation.) Click Next to continue with the installation.

5. Click Next to accept the default settings.

6. On the Destination Folder page, click Next to accept the default folder destination.

7. On the Choose Install Options page, clear the Place Shortcut On The Desktop, Show Readme File After Installation, and Launch Application After Installation check boxes, and then click Next.

8. On the Select Features page, click Next to accept the default settings.

9. On the Ready To Install The Application page, click Next to begin the installation.

   When the installation is completed, the Microsoft Baseline Security Analyzer Has Been Successfully Installed page appears.

10. Click Finish to close the wizard.

Scanning Computers with MBSA

IMPORTANT *Complete this task from both student computers. This will allow you to scan your computer with MBSA to locate security vulnerabilities.*

1. Start your computer running Windows Server 2003, and log on as **administrator@***domain***.contoso.com** (where *domain* is the name of your domain).

2. Click Start, point to All Programs, and then click Microsoft Baseline Security Analyzer to open the Microsoft Baseline Security Analyzer window.

3. In the left pane, click the Pick A Computer To Scan link to open the Pick A Computer To Scan page in the right pane.

    By default, MBSA is configured to scan only the local computer.

4. Click the Start Scan link at the bottom of the page to allow MBSA to begin scanning the computer; when it is finished, it displays the View Security Report page.

5. Close the MBSA window.

    QUESTION   List the potential security vulnerabilities of your computer as disclosed by MBSA.

Using Mbsacli.exe

IMPORTANT   Complete this task from both student computers. This will allow you to use the Mbsacli utility to scan your computer for security vulnerabilities. To receive complete feedback, student computers must have Internet access.

1. Start your computer running Windows Server 2003, and log on as **student*xx*@*domain*.contoso.com** (where student*xx* is your student User Name and *domain* is the name of your domain).

2. Click Start, and then click Run to open the Run window.

3. In the Open box, type **cmd**, and then click OK.

4. In the Cmd.exe window, at the command prompt, type **cd**, and then press ENTER.

5. At the C command prompt, type **cd c:\program files\microsoft baseline security analyzer**.

6. At the C:\Program Files\Microsoft Baseline Security Analyzer command prompt, type **mbsacli /?**.

    QUESTION   What is the description for Mbsacli.exe?

7. At the C:\Program Files\Microsoft Baseline Security Analyzer command prompt, type **mbsacli**, and then press ENTER.

    Record the scan results below:

    _____

    _____

    _____

    _____

8. Close the command prompt window.

LAB REVIEW QUESTIONS

1. Where is auditing of security events enabled?

2. How can documents be encrypted for users whose files are stored on file servers on the network?

3. What are some methods for encrypting files either locally, across the network, or both?

4. Name three switches that are available for the Mbsacli utility.

5. What happens when you run the Mbsacli utility with no parameters?

LAB CHALLENGE 5-1: WINGTIP TOYS SECURITY PLAN

Estimated completion time: 30 minutes

You are a network administrator for Wingtip Toys, and you have been asked to upgrade the security for your domain. Specifically, you must encrypt a folder named Profits, which is located on your C drive. (You will need to create a folder named Profits.) Designate your partner's computer as the recovery agent. Additionally, you must compare the current security settings against the predefined Hisecdc security template; you will do this from the command line. When you have completed the comparison, apply a predefined security template that provides a medium level of security, which still allows for communication with pre–Microsoft Windows 2000 clients.

SECURING NETWORK TRAFFIC BY USING IPSEC

This lab contains the following exercises and activities:

■ Exercise 6-1: Blocking TCP/IP Traffic by Using IPSec

■ Exercise 6-2: Encrypting FTP Traffic by Using IPSec

■ Exercise 6-3: Managing IPSec Policies

■ Exercise 6-4: Monitoring and Troubleshooting IPSec

■ Exercise 6-5: Removing IPSec Policies

■ Lab Review Questions

■ Lab Challenge 6-1: Protecting HTTP Data by Using IPSec

SCENARIO

You are the network administrator for Northwind Traders. You have installed and deployed two internal Microsoft Internet Information Server (IIS) 6 Web servers for use by employees of the company. These internal Web servers will host internal File Transfer Protocol (FTP) sites that will be used by certain employees to store and retrieve secure and confidential company data. You must ensure that only FTP traffic is allowed and that the FTP traffic is encrypted while it is being transmitted across the network.

After completing this lab, you will be able to:

■ Manage and secure network traffic using Internet Protocol Security (IPSec).

■ Monitor and troubleshoot IPSec traffic and connections.

Estimated completion time: 130 minutes

EXERCISE 6-1: BLOCKING TCP/IP TRAFFIC BY USING IPSEC

Estimated completion time: 30 minutes

You are concerned that users will try to access the FTP servers using an unsecure method. You want to ensure that they specifically do not try to use Web Distributed Authoring and Versioning (WebDAV) over Hypertext Transfer Protocol (HTTP) or HTTP to access the Web server using unsecured communications. In this exercise, you must configure IPSec policies to block all HTTP traffic to an FTP server in the Research department.

Installing the WWW and FTP Services

IMPORTANT   *Complete this task from both student computers. This will allow you to install the FTP service on your server computer that runs Microsoft Windows Server 2003. This exercise will verify that you can communicate with your partner's computer using HTTP and FTP.*

1. Start your computer running Windows Server 2003, and log on as **student*xx*@*domain*.contoso.com** (where student*xx* is your student User Name and *domain* is the name of your domain).

2. Click Start, and then select Control Panel.

3. While holding the SHIFT key, right-click Add Or Remove Programs, and then click Run As to open the Run As dialog box.

4. In the Run As dialog box, select The Following User option, and then enter the following credentials in the dialog box fields to open the Add Or Remove Programs window:

    a. In the User Name box, enter **administrator@*domain*.contoso.com** (where *domain* is the name of your domain).

    b. In the Password box, enter **MSPress@LS#1**.

5. In the Add Or Remove Programs window, click Add/Remove Windows Components.

6. In the Windows Components Wizard, under Components, select the Application Server option, and then click the Details button.

7. In the Application Server window, select Internet Information Services (IIS), and then click the Details button.

8. In the Internet Information Services (IIS) window, select the File Transfer Protocol (FTP) Service and the World Wide Web Service check boxes, and then click OK.

9. In the Application Server window, click OK.

10. In the Windows Components Wizard, click Next.

11. If asked for the location of the installation files, place the Windows Server 2003 installation CD into the CD-ROM drive, and then click OK.

12. Click Finish in the Completing The Windows Components Wizard window.

13. Close all open windows.

Configuring the WWW and FTP Services

IMPORTANT   *Complete this task from both student computers. This will allow you to configure the WWW and FTP services on your server computer that runs Windows Server 2003.*

1. Start your computer running Windows Server 2003, and log on as **administrator@*domain*.contoso.com** (where *domain* is the name of your domain).

2. Click Start, point to All Programs, select Accessories, and then click Notepad to open Microsoft Notepad.

3. In the Untitled - Notepad window, type the following text:

```
<html>
<head>
<title>Welcome to the World Wide Web</title>
</head>
<body>
<p><font color="#0066CC" face="Arial"><b>This is the default page
    for the World Wide Web service!!</b></font></p>
</body>
</html>
```

4. In the Untitled - Notepad window, click File, and then click Save As.

5. In the Save As window, click My Computer on the left, and then navigate to the C:\Inetpub\Wwwroot folder.

6. In the Save As window, in the File Name box, type **default.htm**, and then click Save to save the Default.htm file to the C:\Inetpub\Wwwroot folder.

7. In the Default.htm - Notepad window, in a new line, type **This is a file that is stored in the FTP directory**.

8. In the Default.htm - Notepad window, click File, and then click Save As.

9. In the Save As window, click My Computer in the left pane, and then navigate to the C:\Inetpub\Ftproot folder.

10. In the Save As window, in the File Name box, type **ftpfile**, and then click Save to save the Ftpfile.txt file to the C:\Inetpub\Ftproot folder.

11. Close the Notepad window.

12. Click Start, point to All Programs, and then click Internet Explorer.

13. In the Microsoft Internet Explorer Address bar, type **http://computer.xx** (where computer.xx is the name of your partner's computer), and then press ENTER. (If you are asked for credentials, use the administrator account and password.)

QUESTION   Which page appears in the Internet Explorer window?

14. In the Internet Explorer Address bar, type **ftp://computer.xx** (where computer.xx is the name of your partner's computer), and then press ENTER.

QUESTION   Which file appears in the Internet Explorer window?

15. Close all open windows.

Creating an IPSec MMC Console

IMPORTANT   Complete this task from both student computers. This will allow you to create a Microsoft Management Console (MMC) with IPSec snap-ins. You will use it to create and assign IPSec policies to a server computer that runs Windows Server 2003.

1. Start your computer running Windows Server 2003, and log on as **administrator@domain.contoso.com** (where *domain* is the name of your domain).

2. Click Start, click Run, in the Open box, type **mmc**, and then press ENTER to open the MMC.

3. To add an MMC snap-in to the console, click the File menu, and then click Add/Remove Snap-In.

4. In the Add/Remove Snap-In window, click the Add button.

5. In the Add Standalone Snap-In window, click IP Security Policy Management, and then click Add.

6. In the Select Computer Or Domain window, click Local Computer, and then click Finish.

7. In the Add Standalone Snap-In window, click Close.

8. In the Add/Remove Snap-In window, click OK.

9. On the menu bar, click File, click Save As, and then click Desktop.

10. In the File Name box, type **ipsec**, and then click Save.

11. Close all open windows.

Viewing IPSec Statistics

IMPORTANT   Complete this task from both student computers. This will allow you to view IPSec statistics on your server computer that runs Windows Server 2003.

1. Start your computer running Windows Server 2003, and log on as **administrator@domain.contoso.com** (where *domain* is the name of your domain).

2. Click Start, click Run, in the Open box, type **cmd**, and then press Enter.

3. At the command prompt, type **netsh ipsec dynamic show all**, and then press Enter.

   QUESTION Have any IPSec policies been assigned to this computer?

4. Close all open windows.

Creating and Assigning an IPSec Blocking Policy

IMPORTANT Complete this task from both student computers. IPSec policies can be used to block specific Internet Protocol (IP)–based traffic; such policies are similar in function to creating packet filters. This will allow you to create and assign an IPSec policy that will block Web server HTTP traffic to a server that runs Windows Server 2003.

1. Start your computer running Windows Server 2003, and log on as **administrator@*domain*.contoso.com** (where *domain* is the name of your domain).

2. On the desktop, double-click Ipsec.msc to open the IPSec console.

3. In the IPSec console tree, select IP Security Policies On Local Computer, click the Action menu, and then click Create IP Security Policy to launch the IP Security Policy Wizard.

4. On the Welcome page, click Next.

5. On the IP Security Policy Name page, in the Name box, type **block http traffic**, and then click Next.

6. On the Requests For Secure Communication page, clear the Activate The Default Response Rule option, and then click Next.

   QUESTION What does disabling the default response rule accomplish?

7. On the Completing The IP Security Policy Wizard page, click Finish.

   The Block HTTP Traffic Properties page appears.

8. In the Rules tab on the Block HTTP Traffic Properties page, clear the Use Add Wizard option, and then click the Add button.

9. In the IP Filter List tab on the New Rule Properties page, click the Add button.

   The IP Filter List page appears.

10. On the IP Filter List page, in the Name box, type **blocking http**, clear the Use Add Wizard option, and then click the Add button to add a filter.

11. In the IP Filter Properties page, in the Source Address drop-down list, select Any IP Address.

12. In the IP Filter Properties page, in the Destination Address drop-down list, select My IP Address, and then click the Protocol tab.

13. In the Protocol tab on the IP Filter Properties page, in the Select A Protocol Type drop-down list, select TCP.

14. In the Protocol tab on the IP Filter Properties page, in the Set The IP Protocol Port section, click the To This Port option, type **80**, and then click OK.

   QUESTION Why is choosing port 80 correct?

15. On the IP Filter List page, click OK to confirm your entries.

16. In the IP Filter List tab on the New Rule Properties page, select the Blocking HTTP option from the list, and then click the Filter Action tab.

   QUESTION What does the filter action do?

17. On the New Rule Properties page, clear the Use Add Wizard option, and then click the Add button to add a filter action.

18. In the Security Methods tab on the Filter Actions Properties page, select the Block option.

19. In the General tab of the New Rule Filter Actions Properties page, type **block** for the name of the filter, and then click OK.

20. On the New Rule Properties page, select the IP Filter List tab, and then click Blocking HTTP from the IP Filter Lists section.

21. In the Filter Action tab on the New Rule Properties page, select the Block option from the Filter Actions list, click Apply, and then click OK.

22. On the Block HTTP Traffic Properties page, verify that the Blocking HTTP option is selected, and then click OK to finish creating the IPSec policy.

23. In the IPSec console details pane, in the Name column, right-click the Block HTTP Traffic IPSec policy, and then click Assign.

24. Close the console and do not save the changes when prompted.

Verifying IPSec Policy Assignment

   IMPORTANT Complete this task from both student computers. This will allow you to view IPSec statistics on your server computer that runs Windows Server 2003.

1. Start your computer running Windows Server 2003, and log on as **administrator@*domain*.contoso.com** (where *domain* is the name of your domain).

2. Click Start, click Run, and in the Open box, type **cmd**, and then press ENTER.

3. At the command prompt, type **netsh ipsec dynamic show all**, and then press ENTER.

   QUESTION Have any IPSec policies been assigned to this computer? (Hint: Look in the command prompt window.)

4. Close all open windows.

Testing the IPSec Blocking Policy

IMPORTANT *Complete this task from both student computers. This will allow you to test HTTP and FTP communications between your server computer that runs Windows Server 2003 and your partner's server computer.*

1. Start your computer running Windows Server 2003, and log on as **administrator@*domain*.contoso.com** (where *domain* is the name of your domain).

2. Click Start, point to All Programs, and then click Internet Explorer.

3. In the Internet Explorer Address bar, type **http://computer*xx*** (where computer*xx* is the name of your partner's computer), and then press ENTER.

   QUESTION   Which page appears in the Internet Explorer window?

4. In the Internet Explorer Address bar, type **ftp://computer*xx*** (where computer*xx* is the name of your partner's computer), and then press ENTER.

   QUESTION   Which file appears in the Internet Explorer window?

5. Double-click Ipsec.msc on your desktop, select IP Security Policies On Local Computer in the scope pane, and in the IPSec console scope pane, click the Block HTTP Traffic IPSec policy.

6. In the details pane, right-click the IPSec policy, and then select Unassign from the shortcut menu.

7. Close all open windows.

EXERCISE 6-2: ENCRYPTING FTP TRAFFIC BY USING IPSEC

Estimated completion time: 30 minutes

You must enable secure FTP access for a group of users on the company network. These network users transfer data to FTP servers in the Product Development department. You are concerned about the lack of security and wish to protect not only the credentials that are used to log on to the FTP servers but also the data that is transmitted across the network. In this exercise, you will verify that the data and credentials that are passed across the network to the FTP servers are secured.

Configuring the FTP Service

IMPORTANT *Complete this task from both student computers. This will allow you to configure the FTP service on your server computer that runs Windows Server 2003.*

1. Start your computer running Windows Server 2003, and log on as **student*xx*@*domain*.contoso.com** (where student*xx* is your student User Name and *domain* is the name of your domain).

2. Click Start, select Control Panel, and then double-click Administrative Tools.

3. Right-click Internet Information Services (IIS) Manager, and then click Run As to open the Run As dialog box.

4. In the Run As dialog box, select The Following User option, and then enter the following credentials in the dialog box fields to open the Internet Information Services (IIS) Manager console:

   a. In the User Name box, enter **administrator@*domain*.contoso.com** (where *domain* is the name of your domain).

   b. In the Password box, enter **MSPress@LS#1**.

5. In the Internet Information Services (IIS) Manager console tree, expand Computer*xx* (where Computer*xx* is the name of your student computer), and then expand FTP Sites.

6. Select the Default FTP Site node, click the Action menu, and then click Properties to open the Default FTP Site Properties window.

7. In the Default FTP Site Properties window, click the Security Accounts tab.

8. In the Security Accounts tab, ensure the Allow Anonymous Connections option is cleared, and then click OK.

9. In the IIS Manager warning dialog box, click Yes to continue.

10. In the Home Directory tab in the Default FTP Site Properties window, under the FTP Site Directory section, select the Write check box.

11. Click OK to accept your changes.

12. Close all open windows.

Installing Network Monitor

IMPORTANT Complete this task from both student computers. This will allow you to install Network Monitor on your server computer that runs Windows Server 2003. It will be used to inspect network packets that are received by your server.

1. Start your computer running Windows Server 2003, and log on as **administrator@*domain*.contoso.com** (where *domain* is the name of your domain).

2. Click Start, select Control Panel, and then click Add Or Remove Programs.

3. In the Add Or Remove Programs window, click Add/Remove Windows Components.

4. On the Windows Components page, under Components, select the Management And Monitoring Tools option, and then click the Details button.

5. In the Management And Monitoring Tools window, select the Network Monitor Tools check box, and then click OK.

6. On the Windows Components page, click Next.

7. If asked for the location of the installation files, place the Windows Server 2003 installation CD into the CD-ROM drive, then click OK.

8. On the Completing The Windows Components Wizard window, click Finish.

9. Close all open windows.

Capturing FTP Clear-Text Credentials

IMPORTANT   *Complete this task from both student computers. This will allow you to capture the credentials used to open a session with the FTP service.*

1. Start your computer running Windows Server 2003, and log on as **administrator@*domain*.contoso.com** (where *domain* is the name of your domain).

2. Click Start, select Administrative Tools, and then click Network Monitor.

3. If prompted for the network, click the Contoso Ltd Network adapter, and then click OK.

4. In the Microsoft Network Monitor window, click Capture from the menu bar, and then click Start.

5. Click Start, point to All Programs, and then click Internet Explorer.

6. In the Internet Explorer window Address box, type **ftp://computer.*xx*** (where computer.*xx* is the name of your partner's computer), and then press ENTER.

7. In the Log On As window, enter the following credentials:

    a. In the User Name box, type **administrator**.

    b. In the Password box, type **MSPress@LS#1**.

8. In the Log On As window, click the Log On button.

IMPORTANT   *Wait for your partner to complete the preceding steps before stopping the capture.*

9. In the Microsoft Network Monitor window, click Capture from the menu bar, and then click Stop And View.

10. In the Microsoft Network Monitor window, in the Capture: 1 (Summary) window, click Display from the menu bar, and then click Filter.

11. In the Display Filter window, click the Protocol = = Any option, and then click Edit Expression.

12. In the Protocol tab in the Expression window, click the Disable All button.

13. In the Disabled Protocols section, select FTP, click the Enable button, and then click OK.

14. In the Display Filter window, click OK.

15. In the Description column, locate the user account used to log on to the FTP server. (Hint: Look for administrator and the password in the description column.) Record the results below:

   a. User: _____

   b. Password: _____

   QUESTION   *Why are the credentials in clear text?*

16. Close the Microsoft Network Monitor window.

17. In the Microsoft Network Monitor dialog box, when you are prompted to save the capture, click No.

Capturing FTP Clear-Text Data

IMPORTANT   *Complete this task from both student computers. This will allow you to start Network Monitor and capture clear-text FTP data on your server computer that runs Windows Server 2003.*

1. Start your computer running Windows Server 2003, and log on as **administrator@*domain*.contoso.com** (where *domain* is the name of your domain).

2. On your desktop, right-click an open area, select New, and then click Text Document.

3. For the file name, type **unencryptedfile.txt**.

4. Double-click the UnencryptedFile.txt to open it in Notepad.

5. In the UnencryptedFile.txt file, type **here is my clear text**.

6. Click File from the menu bar, click Exit, and then, when prompted to save changes, click Yes.

7. Click Start, click Administrative Tools, and then click Network Monitor.

8. If prompted for the network, click the Contoso Ltd Network adapter, and then click OK.

9. In the Microsoft Network Monitor window, click Capture from the menu bar, and then click Start.

10. Click Start, point to All Programs, and then click Internet Explorer.

11. In the Internet Explorer window Address box, type **ftp://computer.*xx*** (where computer.*xx* is the name of your partner's computer).

12. In the Log On As window, enter the following credentials:

   a. In the User Name box, type **administrator**.

   b. In the Password box, type **MSPress@LS#1**.

13. In the Log On As window, click the Log On button.

14. Drag the UnencryptedFile.txt into the Internet Explorer window for Ftp://Computer.*xx* (where Computer.*xx* is the name of your partner's computer), and then click Copy Here.

   IMPORTANT Wait for your partner to complete the preceding steps before stopping the capture.

15. In the Microsoft Network Monitor window, click Capture from the menu bar, and then click Stop And View.

16. In the Microsoft Network Monitor window, in the Capture: 1 (Summary) window, click Display from the menu bar, and then click Filter.

17. In the Display Filter window, click the Protocol = = Any option, and then click Edit Expression.

18. In the Protocol tab of the Expression window, click the Disable All button.

19. In the Disabled Protocols section, select FTP, click the Enable button, and then click OK.

20. In the Display Filter window, click OK.

21. In the Microsoft Network Monitor window, Capture: 1 (Summary) window, in the Description column, locate STOR UnencryptedFile.txt.

   QUESTION Is this the name of the file that you transferred using FTP?

Creating an IPSec Policy to Encrypt Data Between Two Computers

   IMPORTANT Complete this task from the student computer with the lower number. When configuring IPSec, this computer will act as the IPSec server. This task will allow you to begin the process of protecting the FTP traffic using IPSec. The IP filter list you create enables the computers to protect only the traffic you select, which in this case is FTP traffic.

1. Start your computer running Windows Server 2003, and log on as **administrator@*domain*.contoso.com** (where *domain* is the name of your domain).

2. On the desktop, double-click Ipsec.msc to open the IPSec console.

3. In the IPSec console, right-click IP Security Policies On Local Computer, and then select Create IP Security Policy.

   The IP Security Policy Wizard opens.

4. On the Welcome To The IP Security Policy Wizard page, click Next.

5. On the IP Security Policy Name page, in the Name box, type **EncryptFTP**, and then click Next.

6. On the Request For Secure Communication page, clear the Activate The Default Response Rule option, and then click Next.

7. On the Completing The IP Security Policy Wizard page, click Finish.

8. On the EncryptFTP Properties page, in the Rules tab, ensure the Use Add Wizard check box is selected, and then click Add to add a new rule.

9. On the Welcome To The Create IP Security Rule Wizard page, click Next.

10. On the Tunnel Endpoint page, verify that the This Rule Does Not Specify A Tunnel option is selected, and then click Next.

11. On the Network Type page, verify that the All Network Connections option is selected, and then click Next.

QUESTION   What does selecting the All Network Connections option do?

12. On the IP Filter List page, click Add to add a filter list.

13. On the IP Filter List page, type **ftp (negotiate)**, ensure the Use Add Wizard check box is selected, and then click Add to add a filter.

The IP Filter Wizard opens.

14. On the Welcome To The IP Filter Wizard page, click Next.

15. On the IP Filter Description And Mirrored Property page, in the Description box, type **ftp encryption filter**, and then click Next.

16. On the IP Traffic Source page, in the Source Address drop-down list, select Any IP Address, and then click Next.

17. On the IP Traffic Destination page, in the Destination Address drop-down list, select My IP Address, and then click Next.

18. On the IP Protocol Type page, in the Select A Protocol Type drop-down list, click TCP, and then click Next.

19. On the IP Protocol Port page, select the To This Port option, in the To This Port box, type **21**, click Next, and then click Finish.

QUESTION   Why is port 21 used?

20. In the IP Filter List dialog box, click OK to return to the IP Filter List page.

21. On the IP Filter List page, select the FTP (Negotiate) option, and then click Next.

22. On the Filter Action page, select the Require Security option, and then click Next.

23. On the Authentication Method page, verify that the Active Directory Default (Kerberos V5 Protocol) option is selected, and then click Next.

24. On the Completing The Security Rule Wizard page, clear the Edit Properties option, and then click Finish.

25. On the EncryptFTP Properties page, clear the Use Add Wizard option, and then click OK to finish creating the rule.

26. In the IPSec MMC console details pane, in the Name column, right-click the EncryptFTP IPSec Policy, and then click Assign.

27. Close all open windows.

Clearing the IKE (Internet Key Exchange) State: Restarting the IPSec Policy Agent Service

IMPORTANT Complete this task from the student computer with the lower number. This will allow you to stop and restart the Policy Agent service to ensure that the IPSec filter is activated.

1. Start your computer running Windows Server 2003, and log on as **administrator@*domain*.contoso.com** (where *domain* is the name of your domain).

2. Click Start, click Run, in the Open box, type **cmd**, and then press ENTER.

3. At the command prompt, type **net stop policyagent**, and then press ENTER to stop the IPSec-related services.

4. At the command prompt, type **net start policyagent**, and then press ENTER to restart the IPSec-related services.

5. In the command prompt window, type **exit**, and then press ENTER to close the command prompt window.

Capturing FTP Encrypted Data and Credentials

IMPORTANT Complete this task from the student computer with the lower number. This will allow you to capture the packets that are received by the network adapter on your student computer.

1. Start your computer running Windows Server 2003, and log on as **administrator@*domain*.contoso.com** (where *domain* is the name of your domain).

2. Click Start, click Administrative Tools, and then click Network Monitor.

3. In the Microsoft Network Monitor window, click Capture from the menu bar, and then click Start.

IMPORTANT Complete the following tasks from the student computer with the higher number. This will allow you to configure the student computer to act as the IPSec client.

1. Start your computer running Windows Server 2003, and log on as **administrator@*domain*.contoso.com** (where *domain* is the name of your domain).

2. On the desktop, double-click Ipsec.msc to open the IPSec console.

3. In the IPSec console scope pane, double-click IP Security Policies On Local Computer, right-click the Client (Respond Only) IPSec policy, and then click Assign.

4. Close all windows.

5. Click Start, click Run, in the Open box, type **cmd**, and then press ENTER.

6. In the command prompt window, type **net stop policyagent**, and then press ENTER.

7. In the command prompt window, type **net start policyagent**, and then press ENTER.

8. In the command prompt window, type **exit** to close the command prompt window.

9. Right-click the desktop, click New, and then select Text Document.

10. For the file name, type **encryptedfile.txt**.

11. Double-click EncryptedFile.txt to open it in Notepad.

12. In the EncryptedFile.txt file, type **Here is my encrypted data**.

13. Click File from the menu bar, click Exit, and, when prompted to save changes, click Yes.

14. Click Start, point to All Programs, and then click Internet Explorer.

15. In the Internet Explorer window Address box, type **ftp://computer*xx***
(where computer*xx* is the name of your partner's computer).

16. In the Log On As window, enter the following credentials:

   a. In the User Name box, type **administrator**.

   b. In the Password box, type **MSPress@LS#1**.

17. In the Log On As window, click the Log On button.

18. Drag the EncryptedFile.txt into the Internet Explorer window for Ftp://Computer*xx* (where Computer*xx* is the name of your partner's computer), and then click Copy Here.

   IMPORTANT   Complete the following tasks from the student computer with the lower number. This will allow you to capture the packets that are received by the network adapter on your student computer.

1. In the Microsoft Network Monitor window, click Capture from the menu bar, and then click Stop And View.

2. In the Microsoft Network Monitor window, in the Capture: 1 (Summary) window, click Display from the menu bar, and then click Filter.

3. In the Display Filter window, click the Protocol = = Any option, and then click Edit Expression.

4. In the Protocol tab in the Expression window, click the Disable All button.

5. In the Disabled Protocols section, select FTP, click the Enable button, and then click OK.

6. In the Display Filter window, click OK.

   QUESTION   *Are any FTP protocol packets captured? Why?*

7. In the Microsoft Network Monitor window, in the Capture: 1 (Summary) window, click Display from the menu bar, and then click Filter.

8. In the Display Filter window, click the Protocol = = FTP option, then click Edit Expression.

9. In the Protocol tab in the Expression window, click the Disable All button.

10. In the Disabled Protocols section, select ESP, click the Enable button, and then click OK.

11. In the Display Filter window, click OK. Double-click an entry to open the hex-pane.

    QUESTION   *Can you recognize the data in the hex-pane of the data in the packets that were captured?*

12. Close all open windows.

    QUESTION   *Does IPSec encrypt both the clear-text credentials and the data that are transmitted across the network?*

EXERCISE 6-3: MANAGING IPSEC POLICIES

Estimated completion time: 10 minutes

You must configure the same IPSec policies you have created for your FTP server on another FTP server in the Sales department.

Exporting an IPSec Policy

IMPORTANT   *Complete this task from the student computer with the lower number. This will allow you to export to another computer the IPSec policy you initially created.*

1. Start your computer running Windows Server 2003, and log on as **administrator@*domain*.contoso.com** (where *domain* is the name of your domain).

2. On the desktop, right-click an open area, select New, and then click Folder to create a new folder.

3. Enter **ipsec** as the folder name.

4. Right-click the Ipsec folder on your desktop, and then click Sharing And Security from the shortcut menu.

5. In the Sharing tab on the Ipsec Properties page, click Share This Folder, and then click OK.

6. On the desktop, double-click Ipsec.msc to open the IPSec console.

7. In the IPSec console tree, right-click IP Security Policies On Local Computer, click All Tasks, and then click Export Policies.

8. In the Save As window, click Desktop, and then double-click the Ipsec shared folder.

9. In the File Name box, type **encryptftp**, and then click Save.

10. In the IPSec console tree, right-click the IP Security Policies On Local Computer, click All Tasks, and then click Restore Default Policies.

11. In the IP Security Policy Management dialog box, click Yes, and then click OK.

12. Close all open windows.

Importing an IPSec Policy

IMPORTANT   Complete this task from the student computer with the higher number. This will allow you to import the FTP IPSec policy from your partner's computer.

1. Start your computer running Windows Server 2003, and log on as **administrator@_domain_.contoso.com** (where _domain_ is the name of your domain).

2. On the desktop, double-click Ipsec.msc MMC to open the IPSec console.

3. In the IPSec console tree, right-click the IP Security Policies On Local Computer, click All Tasks, and then click Restore Default Policies.

4. In the IP Security Policy Management warning box, click Yes, and then click OK.

5. Click Start, click Run, and then type **computer_xx_\ipsec** (where computer_xx_ is the name of your partner's computer) in the Open box.

6. Drag the EncryptFtp.Ipsec file to the desktop, and then select Copy Here.

7. In the IPSec console tree, right-click IP Security Policies On Local Computer, click All Tasks, and then click Import Policies.

8. In the Open window, click Desktop, click the EncryptFtp.Ipsec file, and then click Open.

QUESTION   Which TCP port has been configured on the EncryptFtp IPSec filter on your student computer?

Assigning and Unassigning IPSec Policies

IMPORTANT   Complete this task from the student computer with the lower number. This will allow you to unassign the IPSec policies on your student computer.

1. Start your computer running Windows Server 2003, and log on as **administrator@_domain_.contoso.com** (where _domain_ is the name of your domain).

2. On the desktop, double-click the Ipsec.msc MMC console file to open the IPSec console.

3. In the IPSec console details pane, right-click the EncryptFtp IPSec policy, and then click Un-Assign.

4. In the IPSec details pane, select and right-click the Client (Respond Only) IPSec policy, and then click Assign.

5. Close all open windows.

> **IMPORTANT** *Complete the following tasks from the student computer with the higher number. This will allow you to unassign the IPSec policies on your student computer.*

1. Start your computer running Windows Server 2003, and log on as **administrator@domain.contoso.com** (where *domain* is the name of your domain).

2. On the desktop, double-click Ipsec.msc to open the IPSec console.

3. In the IPSec console details pane, right-click the Client (Respond Only) IPSec policy, and then click Un-Assign.

4. In the IPSec console scope pane, click the Server (Request Security) IPSec policy, and then click Assign.

5. Close all open windows.

EXERCISE 6-4: MONITORING AND TROUBLESHOOTING IPSEC

Estimated completion time: 15 minutes

After installing and configuring IPSec for FTP servers on your internal network, you must be able to use IPSec tools and utilities to monitor and troubleshoot IPSec connections to the FTP servers on the internal network. In this exercise, you will use built-in IPSec tools to monitor and troubleshoot the IPSec connections.

Enabling IKE Debug Tracing

> **IMPORTANT** *Complete this task from the student computer with the higher number. This will allow you to enable logging in an Oakley log. It can be enabled by modifying the registry.*

1. Start your computer running Windows Server 2003, and log on as **administrator@domain.contoso.com** (where *domain* is the name of your domain).

2. Click Start, click Run, in the Open box, type **regedt32**, and then click OK to open Registry Editor.

3. In the Registry Editor console, navigate to and expand HKEY_LOCAL_MACHINE.

4. In the HKEY_LOCAL_MACHINE registry key, navigate to the following location: System\CurrentControlSet\Services\PolicyAgent.

5. Expand the PolicyAgent subkey.

6. In the console tree, locate and select the Oakley registry subkey.

7. On the Edit menu, click New, and then click DWORD Value.

8. In the New Value #1 box, enter the Value Name (which is case-sensitive) **EnableLogging**, and then press ENTER.

9. In the details pane, right-click DWORD Enable Logging, and then click Modify.

10. In the Edit DWORD Value dialog box, in the Value Data box, type **1**, and then click OK.

   QUESTION   What would happen if you entered 0 for the value data for EnableLogging?

11. Close the Registry Editor.

12. Click Start, click Run, in the Open box, type **cmd**, and then press ENTER.

13. At the command prompt, type **net stop policyagent**, and then press ENTER to stop the IPSec-related services.

14. At the command prompt, type **net start policyagent**, and then press ENTER to restart the IPSec-related services.

15. In the command prompt window, type **exit** to close the command prompt window.

   The Oakley log file will be written to the %systemroot%\Debug\Oakley.log file by default, and the file Oakley.log.sav is the previous version of the log after the Policy Agent service is restarted.

16. Close all open windows.

Viewing IPSec Statistics with the IPSec Monitor MMC Snap-In

   IMPORTANT   Complete this task from both student computers. This will allow you to view IPSec statistics using IPSec Monitor.

1. Start your computer running Windows Server 2003, and log on as **administrator@*domain*.contoso.com** (where *domain* is the name of your domain).

2. On the desktop, double-click Ipsec.msc to open the IPSec console.

3. In the IPSec console, click File, and then click Add/Remove Snap-In to open the Add/Remove Snap-In window.

4. In the Add/Remove Snap-In window, click Add.

5. In the Add Standalone Snap-In window, click IP Security Monitor, click Add, and then click Close.

6. In the Add/Remove Snap-In window, click OK.

7. In the IPSec console tree, expand IP Security Monitor, and then expand Computer*xx* (where Computer*xx* is the name of your computer).

   QUESTION   Does your student computer have any security associations established? If so, with whom? (Hint: Look in the Main Mode section under Security Associations.)

8. Close all open windows.

9. When prompted to save your IPSec MMC console settings, click Yes.

Using Netsh to View IPSec Statistics

IMPORTANT *Complete this task from both student computers. This will allow you to view IPSec statistics using Netsh.*

1. Start your computer running Windows Server 2003, and log on as **administrator@*domain*.contoso.com** (where *domain* is the name of your domain).

2. Click Start, click Run, in the Open box, type **cmd**, and then press ENTER.

3. At the command prompt, type **netsh ipsec static show policy all >c:\ipsec.txt**.

4. Click Start, and then click My Computer to open the My Computer window.

5. In the My Computer window, locate and then double-click the C drive.

6. In the C drive window, double-click the Ipsec.txt file to open it.

   QUESTION How many IPSec policies are assigned?

   QUESTION How many IPSec policies are on the local computer?

Viewing the Oakley Log IPSec Statistics

IMPORTANT *Complete this task from the student computer with the higher number. This will allow you to view IPSec statistics using the Oakley log file.*

1. Start your computer running Windows Server 2003, and log on as **administrator@*domain*.contoso.com** (where *domain* is the name of your domain).

2. Click Start, and then click My Computer to open the My Computer window.

3. In the My Computer window, navigate to the %systemroot%\Debug\Oakley.log file.

4. Double-click the Oakley.log file to open it.

   QUESTION Is the EncryptFTP policy currently assigned?

5. Close all open windows.

EXERCISE 6-5: REMOVING IPSEC POLICIES

Estimated completion time: 5 minutes

In this exercise, you will remove the IPSec policies that were created and configured in the previous exercises. Doing so will remove any dependencies that may influence subsequent lab exercises.

Removing IPSec Policies by Using Netsh

IMPORTANT   *Complete this task from both student computers. This will allow you to remove the IPSec policies that were created.*

1. Start your computer running Windows Server 2003, and log on as **administrator@***domain***.contoso.com** (where *domain* is the name of your domain).

2. Click Start, click Run, in the Open box, type **cmd**, and then press ENTER.

3. At the command prompt, type **netsh ipsec static delete policy all**.

4. Close all open windows.

Restoring Default IPSec Policies

IMPORTANT   *Complete this task from both student computers. This will allow you to restore the default IPSec policies on your student computer.*

1. Start your computer running Windows Server 2003, and log on as **administrator@***domain***.contoso.com** (where *domain* is the name of your domain).

2. On the desktop, double-click Ipsec.msc to open the IPSec console.

3. In the IPSec console tree, select and then right-click IP Security Policies On Local Computer, click All Tasks, and then click Restore Default Policies.

4. In the IP Security Policy Management dialog box, click Yes, and then click OK.

5. Close all open windows.

Clearing the IKE (Internet Key Exchange) State: Restarting the IPSec Policy Agent Service

IMPORTANT   *Complete this task from both student computers. This will allow you to stop and restart the IPSec services on your computer.*

1. Start your computer running Windows Server 2003, and log on as **administrator@***domain***.contoso.com** (where *domain* is the name of your domain).

2. Click Start, click Run, in the Open box, type **cmd**, and then press ENTER.

3. At the command prompt, type **net stop policyagent**, and then press ENTER to stop the IPSec-related services.

4. At the command prompt, type **net start policyagent**, and then press ENTER to restart the IPSec-related services.

5. In the command prompt window, type **exit** to close the command prompt window.

LAB REVIEW QUESTIONS

Estimated completion time: 15 minutes

1. What are two methods in which IPSec policies can be used to provide protection for credentials, data, and servers?

2. What is one reason that you would want to use local computer IPSec policies?

3. What are two utilities that can be used to verify that IPSec policies are being applied to the local computer?

4. Describe the process that would use certificate authentication to implement encryption for telnet traffic between one client and multiple telnet servers.

5. How can you configure an IPSec policy to use only Triple DES Secure Hash Algorithm version 1 (3DES SHA1) for encryption?

6. Describe what a preshared key is and why it is not the recommended method of authentication for IPSec.

7. How do the predefined IPSec security policies Secure Server (Require Security) and Server (Request Security) differ from each other?

8. When is it appropriate to use transport mode and when is it appropriate to use tunnel mode?

9. When troubleshooting IPSec, how can you determine whether a problem in communication between two computers is caused by IPSec settings or by general network hardware problems?

LAB CHALLENGE 6-1: PROTECTING HTTP DATA BY USING IPSEC

Estimated completion time: 25 minutes

You are a security administrator for Litware, Inc. Several full-time Web employees need to update information on and download information from the same Windows Server 2003 Web server. All Web employees use Microsoft Windows XP Professional computers, which are all located on the same IP subnet. Your internal network is secured using the Routing and Remote Access basic firewall and Network Address Translation (NAT), but the network has been configured to pass User Datagram Protocol (UDP) ESP traffic. The credentials and data that are transmitted by HTTP must use the highest level of encryption and a secure level of authentication. Your network does not run Certificate Services, but you have considered installing a CA; however, you do not want the additional administrative load, so you are looking for a different solution. Management has told you that the cost of a commercial certificate or third-party certificate that could be installed on the Web server to support Hypertext Transfer Protocol Secure (HTTPS) is prohibitive. How can you configure the Web server to allow secure communications for the Web employees?

LAB 7
IMPLEMENTING AND MANAGING SOFTWARE UPDATE SERVICES

This lab contains the following exercises and activities:

■ Exercise 7-1: Installing, Configuring, and Managing a SUS Server

■ Exercise 7-2: Creating a SUS Hierarchy

■ Exercise 7-3: Managing SUS Client Updates

■ Exercise 7-4: Uninstalling SUS

■ Lab Review Questions

■ Lab Challenge 7-1: Creating a SUS Hierarchy

After completing this lab, you will be able to:

■ Install, configure, and manage a Software Update Services (SUS) server.

■ Configure SUS client computers.

■ Verify client update installations.

■ Back up and restore a SUS server.

■ Configure and create a SUS hierarchy.

Estimated completion time: 115 minutes (This estimate includes the Before You Begin setup procedure.)

BEFORE YOU BEGIN

> **IMPORTANT**   If you have not completed the exercises in Lab 6, "Securing Network Traffic by Using IPSec," you must complete the following prerequisite procedure.

Estimated completion time: 5 minutes

Installing the WWW Service

> **IMPORTANT**   Complete this task from both student computers. This will allow you to install the WWW service on your server computer that runs Microsoft Windows Server 2003.

1. Start your computer running Windows Server 2003, and log on as **student*xx*@*domain*.contoso.com** (where student*xx* is your student User Name and *domain* is the name of your domain).

2. Click Start, and then select Control Panel.

3. While holding down the SHIFT key, right-click Add Or Remove Programs, and then click Run As to open the Run As dialog box.

4. In the Run As dialog box, select The Following User option, and then enter the following credentials in the dialog box fields to open the Add Or Remove Programs window:

    a. In the User Name box, enter **administrator@*domain*.contoso.com** (where *domain* is the name of your domain).

    b. In the Password box, enter **MSPress@LS#1**.

5. In the Add Or Remove Programs window, click Add/Remove Windows Components.

6. In the Components section in the Windows Components Wizard, select the Application Server option, and then click the Details button.

7. In the Application Server window, select Internet Information Services (IIS), and then click the Details button.

8. In the Internet Information Services (IIS) window, select the World Wide Web Service check box, and then click OK.

9. In the Internet Information Services (IIS) window, click OK.

10. In the Application Server window, click OK.

11. In the Windows Components Wizard page, click Next.

12. If asked for the location of the installation files, place the Windows Server 2003 installation CD into the CD-ROM drive, and then click OK.

13. On the Completing The Windows Components Wizard page, click Finish.

14. Close all open windows.

SCENARIO

You are the network administrator for Adventure Works (*http://www.adventure-works.com*). Your network infrastructure contains one Active Directory parent domain, adventure-works.com, and several Active Directory child domains. Each Active Directory child domain is located in a different physical location. In your most recent Information Services (IS) staff meeting, your staff agreed that patching client and server operating systems manually has become extremely complex and takes a great deal of administrative effort. You must plan, design, and implement a Microsoft SUS infrastructure that includes all of the Active Directory domains in your organization.

EXERCISE 7-1: INSTALLING, CONFIGURING, AND MANAGING A SUS SERVER

Estimated completion time: 30 minutes

> **IMPORTANT**   For you to complete this exercise, you must download SUS with Service Pack 1 (*http://www.microsoft.com/downloads/details.aspx?FamilyId=A7AA96E4-6E41-4F54-972C-AE66A4E4BF6C&displaylang=en*) from either this link or the instructor's network share. Ask your instructor if you need to download SUS from the Internet; the following instructions are written so that you download SUS from a network share created by your instructor.

In each of the domains in your organization, you have decided to deploy at least one, possibly two, Microsoft SUS servers to be used to update client and server computers at each physical location. Each SUS server must be configured to synchronize with Windows Update servers on the Internet and, after the updates have downloaded, to approve those updates for distribution to clients on the network. Finally, you must ensure that after you have installed the SUS server and configured updates, the SUS server is backed up and a practice restore operation is performed.

Installing a SUS Server

> **IMPORTANT**   Complete this task from both student computers. This will allow you to install the Microsoft SUS server component.

1. Start your computer running Windows Server 2003, and log on as **student*xx*@*domain*.contoso.com** (where student*xx* is your student User Name and *domain* is the name of your domain).

2. Locate the SUS10SP1.exe installation file in the network share that the instructor created prior to this exercise.

3. Copy the SUS10SP1.exe installation file to your desktop.

4. Right-click the SUS10SP1.exe file, and then select Run As to launch the setup program.

5. In the Run As dialog box, select The Following User option, and then enter the following credentials in the dialog box fields to open the SUS installation program:

   a. In the User Name box, enter **administrator@*domain*.contoso.com** (where *domain* is the name of your domain).

   b. In the Password box, enter **MSPress@LS#1**.

6. Click OK to start the installation of SUS.

7. On the Welcome To The Microsoft Software Update Services Setup Wizard page, click Next.

8. Review the licenses agreement on the End User License Agreement page, and then select I Accept The Terms Of The License Agreement. (If you do not agree with the terms, you cannot continue this installation.) Click Next.

9. On the Choose Setup Type page, click the Custom option.

10. On the Choose File Locations page, verify that Save The Updates To This Local Folder (C:\SUS\Content\) is selected, and then click Next.

11. On the Language Settings page, click English Only option, and then click Next.

12. On the Handling New Versions Of Previously Approved Updates page, verify that I Will Manually Approve New Versions Of Approved Updates is selected, and then click Next.

13. On the Ready To Install page, click Install to start the SUS installation program.

14. On the Completing The Microsoft Software Update Services Setup Wizard page, click Finish to complete the installation.

15. Close the Microsoft Internet Explorer window; you will open the *http://localhost/susadmin* virtual directory in the next exercise.

   QUESTION   What happens if Internet Information Services (IIS) is not installed or the default Web site does not run and you install SUS?

Configuring IP Address Restrictions to the SUS SUSAdmin Virtual Directory

   IMPORTANT   Complete this task from both student computers. This will allow you to configure an Internet Protocol (IP) address that will be allowed access to the SUSAdmin virtual directory.

1. Start your computer running Windows Server 2003, and log on as **student*xx*@*domain*.contoso.com** (where student*xx* is your student User Name and *domain* is the name of your domain).

2. Click Start, click Control Panel, double-click Administrative Tools, right-click Internet Information Services (IIS) Manager, and then select Run As.

3. In the Run As dialog box, select the The Following User option, and then enter the following credentials in the dialog box fields to open the Internet Information Services (IIS) Manager console:

  a. In the User Name box, enter **administrator@*domain*.contoso.com** (where *domain* is the name of your domain).

  b. In the Password box, enter **MSPress@LS#1**.

4. Click OK to open the Internet Information Services (IIS) Manager console.

5. In the Internet Information Services (IIS) Manager console tree, expand Computer*xx* (where Computer*xx* is the name of your computer), expand Web Sites, and then expand Default Web Site.

6. In the Internet Information Services (IIS) Manager console tree, first select and then right-click the SUSAdmin virtual directory, and then click Properties.

7. In the SUSAdmin Properties window, click the Directory Security tab.

8. In the Directory Security tab, under IP Address And Domain Name Restrictions, click Edit to open the IP Address And Domain Name Restrictions window.

9. In the IP Address And Domain Name Restrictions window, click Denied Access, and then click Add.

10. In the Grant Access window, click Single Computer, in the IP Address box, type **172.16.1.1**, and then click OK.

11. In the IP Address And Domain Name Restrictions window, click OK.

12. In the SUSAdmin Properties window, click OK to accept your changes.

13. Click Start, point to All Programs, and then click Internet Explorer to open Microsoft Internet Explorer.

14. In the Internet Explorer Address bar, type **http://localhost/susadmin**, and then press ENTER.

  QUESTION *Why do you receive the error, "You are not authorized to view this page"?*

15. In the Internet Information Services (IIS) Manager console tree, first select and then right-click the SUSAdmin virtual directory, and then click Properties.

16. In the SUSAdmin Properties window, click the Directory Security tab.

17. In the Directory Security tab, under the IP Address And Domain Name Restrictions, click Edit to open the IP Address And Domain Name Restrictions window.

18. In the IP Address And Domain Name Restrictions window, in the Except The Following section, click the 172.16.1.1 IP address, and then click Remove.

19. In the IP Address And Domain Name Restrictions window, click Granted Access.

20. In the IP Address And Domain Name Restrictions window, click OK to accept your changes.

21. In the SUSAdmin Properties window, click OK to accept your changes.

22. In the Internet Information Services (IIS) Manager console tree, first select and then right-click Computer*xx* (Local Computer) (where Computer*xx* is the name of your computer), click All Tasks from the shortcut menu, and then click Restart IIS.

23. In the Stop/Start/Restart dialog box, click OK to restart IIS.

24. Close the Internet Information Services (IIS) Manager console.

25. Click Start, point to All Programs, and then click Internet Explorer to open Internet Explorer.

26. In the Internet Explorer Address bar, type **http://localhost/susadmin**, and then press ENTER.

27. In the Connect To dialog box, enter the following credentials:

   a. In the User Name box, enter **administrator**.

   b. In the Password box, enter **MSPress@LS#1**.

28. The Microsoft Software Update Services default Web page appears in the Internet Explorer window.

29. Close Internet Explorer.

Configuring the SUS Server

IMPORTANT   Complete this task from both student computers. This will allow you to configure the SUS server.

1. Start your computer running Windows Server 2003, and log on as **student*xx*@*domain*.contoso.com** (where student*xx* is your student User Name and *domain* is the name of your domain).

2. Click Start, point to All Programs, and then click Internet Explorer to open Internet Explorer.

3. In the Internet Explorer Address bar, type **http://localhost/susadmin**, and then press ENTER to display the Microsoft Software Update Services default Web page in the Internet Explorer window.

4. In the Connect To dialog box, enter the following credentials:

   a. In the User Name box, enter **administrator**.

   b. In the Password box, enter **MSPress@LS#1**.

5. In the Microsoft Software Update Services navigation menu, click Set Options.

6. Record the main options that are available in the space below:

_____

_____

_____

_____

_____

7. On the Software Update Services navigation menu, click Synchronize Server.

8. In the main pane of Internet Explorer, click Synchronization Schedule. The Schedule Synchronization—Web Page dialog box will appear.

9. In the Schedule Synchronization—Web Page dialog box, click Synchronize Using This Schedule.

   QUESTION   In the At This Time drop-down menu, why is there an option for 19:00? What time is this?

10. In the At This Time drop-down menu, select 4:00, and then click OK to accept your changes.

    IMPORTANT   To complete the following steps (steps 11 through 19, below), the classroom network must be configured for Internet access.

11. In the main window of Internet Explorer, click Synchronize Now.

12. The SUS server will start to download updates from the Microsoft Windows Update server.

    IMPORTANT   This can take many minutes depending on the number of updates available and the speed of your Internet connection.

13. After the download is completed, in the Software Update Services navigation menu, click Approve Updates.

14. In the Internet Explorer Approve Updates window, select three security update packages, and then click Approve.

15. In the VBScript: Software Update Services dialog box, click Yes, and then click Accept in the Software Update Services—Web Page dialog box.

16. In the VBScript: Software Update Services dialog box, click Yes.

17. Record the three approved updates in space below:

    _____

    _____

    _____

18. On the Microsoft Software Update Services navigation menu, under Other Options, click View Approval Log.

    Record the approved updates that are listed in the approval log in the space below:

    _____

    _____

    _____

19. Close Internet Explorer.

Backing Up a SUS Server Configuration

IMPORTANT Complete this task from both student computers. This will allow you to back up the IIS metabase, which contains the SUSAdmin configuration.

1. Start your computer running Windows Server 2003, and log on as **student*xx*@*domain*.contoso.com** (where student*xx* is your student User Name and *domain* is the name of your domain).

2. Click Start, click Control Panel, double-click Administrative Tools, right-click Internet Information Services (IIS) Manager, and then select Run As.

3. In the Run As dialog box, select The Following User option, and then enter the following credentials in the dialog box fields to open the Internet Information Services (IIS) Manager console:

    a. In the User Name box, enter **administrator@*domain*.contoso.com** (where *domain* is the name of your domain).

    b. In the Password box, enter **MSPress@LS#1**.

4. Click OK to open the Internet Information Services (IIS) Manager console.

5. In the Internet Information Services (IIS) Manager console tree, select and right-click Computer*xx* (where Computer*xx* is the name of your computer).

6. On the shortcut menu, click All Tasks, and then click Backup/Restore Configuration to open the Configuration Backup/Restore window.

7. In the Configuration Backup/Restore window, click Create Backup to open the Configuration Backup window, and then, in the Configuration Backup Name box, type **susbackup**.

8. In the Configuration Backup window, select the Encrypt Backup Using Password check box, in the Password box, enter **susadmin**, and then, in the Confirm Password box, enter **susadmin** again to confirm the password.

9. Click Close to close the Configuration Backup/Restore window.

10. Close the Internet Information Services (IIS) Manager console.

QUESTION   When you use the backup procedure, what exactly are you backing up?

QUESTION   How can you back up the entire SUS configuration, SUS files, and SUS installation?

Restoring a SUS Server Configuration

IMPORTANT Complete this task from both student computers. This will allow you to restore the IIS metabase, which contains the SUSAdmin configuration.

1. Start your computer running Windows Server 2003, and log on as **student*xx*@*domain*.contoso.com** (where student*xx* is your student User Name and *domain* is the name of your domain).

2. Click Start, click Control Panel, double-click Administrative Tools, right-click Internet Information Services (IIS) Manager, and then select Run As.

3. In the Run As dialog box, select The Following User option, and then enter the following credentials in the dialog box fields to open the Internet Information Services (IIS) Manager console:

   a. In the User Name box, enter **administrator@*domain*.contoso.com** (where *domain* is the name of your domain).

   b. In the Password box, enter **MSPress@LS#1**.

4. Click OK to open the Internet Information Services (IIS) Manager console.

5. In the Internet Information Services (IIS) Manager console tree, select and right-click Computer*xx* (where Computer*xx* is the name of your computer).

6. On the shortcut menu, click All Tasks, and then click Backup/Restore Configuration to open the Configuration Backup/Restore window.

7. In the Configuration Backup/Restore window, select the susbackup that you created in the preceding exercise, and then click Restore.

8. In the IIS Manager dialog box, click Yes to restore the IIS metabase.

9. In the Backup Password dialog box, type **susadmin**, and then click OK.

10. In the IIS Manager dialog box that states that the operation completed successfully, click OK.

11. Close all open windows.

EXERCISE 7-2: CREATING A SUS HIERARCHY

Estimated completion time: 10 minutes

In each of your domains in the organization, you deployed at least one (possibly two) SUS servers to be used to update client and server computers at each physical location. Currently, each SUS server in each child domain or network physical location downloads its own updates. This causes two problems: the administrators at the main company network want to control the types of updates that are deployed even in the child domains, and excessive wide area network (WAN) bandwidth is used when retrieving the updates. Also, you now must be able to control the type of updates used in each of the child domains in your organization. You want to control the updates through the SUS server in the adventure-works.com domain in the main office.

Configuring a SUS Hierarchy

IMPORTANT   Complete this task from the student computer with the lower number. This will allow you to configure your computer to retrieve updates from the instructor's computer.

1. Start your computer running Windows Server 2003, and log on as **administrator@*domain*.contoso.com** (where *domain* is the name of your domain).

2. Click Start, point to All Programs, and then click Internet Explorer to open the Internet Explorer window.

3. In the Internet Explorer window, in the Address bar, type **http://localhost/susadmin**, and then press ENTER.

4. In the navigation menu of the Software Updates Services default page, click Set Options.

5. In the Set Options window of Internet Explorer, in the Select Which Server To Synchronize Content From section, select Synchronize From A Local Software Update Services Server, and then, in the Name box, type **instructor01.contoso.com**.

6. Click Apply to apply your changes.

> **IMPORTANT**   Complete the following tasks from the student computer with the higher number. This will allow you to configure your computer to retrieve updates from your partner's computer.

1. Start your computer running Windows Server 2003, and log on as **administrator@*domain*.contoso.com** (where *domain* is the name of your domain).

2. Click Start, point to All Programs, and then click Internet Explorer to open the Internet Explorer window.

3. In the Internet Explorer window, in the Address bar, type **http://localhost/susadmin**, and then press ENTER.

4. In the navigation menu of the Software Updates Services default page, click Set Options.

5. In the Set Options window of Internet Explorer, in the Select Which Server To Synchronize Content From section, select Synchronize From A Local Software Update Services Server, and then, in the Name box, type **computer*xx*.*domain*.contoso.com** (where computer*xx* is the name of your partner's computer and *domain* is the name of your domain).

6. Click Apply to apply your changes.

7. Click OK in the VBScript dialog box.

8. Close all open windows.

EXERCISE 7-3: MANAGING SUS CLIENT UPDATES

Estimated completion time: 30 minutes

After you have designed and installed the server-side components of SUS, you must configure a Group Policy Object (GPO) that will allow client computers in the domain to receive updates from a SUS server that is on-site. After the configurations are made, you must verify that the updates have been applied to client computers in the domain.

Uninstalling SUS

IMPORTANT *Complete this task from the student computer with the higher number. This will allow you to uninstall SUS from a student computer so that it can be used as a SUS client computer.*

1. Start your computer running Microsoft Windows Server 2003, and log on as **student*xx*@*domain*.contoso.com** (where student*xx* is your student User Name and *domain* is the name of your domain).

2. Click Start, and then click Control Panel.

3. While holding down the SHIFT key, right-click the Add Or Remove Programs option, and then click Run As to open the Run As dialog box.

4. In the Run As dialog box, select The Following User option, and then enter the following credentials in the dialog box fields to open the Add Or Remove Programs Wizard:

    a. In the User Name box, enter **administrator@*domain*.contoso.com** (where *domain* is the name of your domain).

    b. In the Password box, enter **MSPress@LS#1**.

5. Click OK to open Add Or Remove Programs.

6. In the Add Or Remove Programs window, in the Currently Installed Programs section, click Microsoft Software Update Services, and then click Remove.

7. In the Add Or Remove Programs dialog box, click Yes to confirm removal of the Microsoft SUS.

8. Close the Add Or Remove Programs window.

Configuring SUS Client Options in Group Policy

IMPORTANT *Complete this task from the student computer with the lower number. This will allow you to configure Windows Update for SUS client computers.*

1. Start your computer running Windows Server 2003, and log on as **student*xx*@*domain*.contoso.com** (where student*xx* is your student User Name and *domain* is the name of your domain).

2. Click Start, click Control Panel, double-click Administrative Tools, right-click Active Directory Users And Computers, and then select Run As.

3. In the Run As dialog box, select the The Following User option, and the enter the following credentials in the dialog box fields to open the Add Or Remove Programs Wizard:

    a. In the User Name box, enter **administrator@*domain*.contoso.com** (where *domain* is the name of your domain).

    b. In the Password box, enter **MSPress@LS#1**.

4. Click OK to open the Active Directory Users And Computers console.

5. In the Active Directory Users And Computers console, select and then right-click *Domain*.Contoso.Com (where *Domain* is the name of your domain), and then click Properties.

6. On the *Domain*.Contoso.Com Properties page, click the Group Policy tab.

7. In the Group Policy tab, click New to add a new GPO. As the name of the GPO, type **software updates**, and then press ENTER.

8. With the Software Updates GPO selected, click Edit to open the Group Policy Object Editor window.

9. In the Group Policy Object Editor scope pane, navigate to Computer Configuration\Administrative Templates\Windows Components, and then select Windows Update.

10. In the Group Policy Object Editor details pane, double-click Configure Automatic Updates to open the Configure Automatic Updates Properties window.

11. In the Configure Automatic Updates Properties window, click Enabled, and in the Configure Automatic Updating drop-down menu, click 2-Notify For Download And Notify For Install, and then click OK to accept your changes.

12. In the Group Policy Object Editor details pane, double-click Specify Intranet Microsoft Update Service Location to open the Specify Intranet Microsoft Update Service Location Properties window.

13. In the Specify Intranet Microsoft Update Service Location Properties window, click Enabled.

14. In the Set The Intranet Update Service For Detecting Updates box, type **http://computer.xx** (where computer.xx is the name of your computer).

15. In the Set The Intranet Statistics Server box, type **http://computer.xx**, and then click OK to accept your changes.

16. In the Group Policy Object Editor details pane, double-click Reschedule Automatic Updates Schedule Installations to open the Reschedule Automatic Updates Schedule Installations Properties window, and then click Enable.

17. In the Reschedule Automatic Updates Schedule Installations Properties window, in the Wait After System Startup (Minutes) section, enter **1 minute**, and then click OK to accept your changes.

18. In the Group Policy Object Editor details pane, double-click the No Auto-Restart For Scheduled Automatic Updates Installations option to open the No Auto-Restart For Scheduled Automatic Updates Installations Properties window.

19. In the No Auto-Restart For Scheduled Automatic Updates Installations Properties window, click Enabled, and then click OK to accept your changes.

20. Close all open windows.

Updating and Viewing Group Policy Settings

IMPORTANT   *Complete this task from both student computers. This will allow you to refresh Group Policy to apply the Windows Update settings that you configured. You will also use built-in Windows Server 2003 utilities to view Group Policy information.*

1. Start your computer running Windows Server 2003, and log on as **administrator@*domain*.contoso.com** (where *domain* is the name of your domain).

2. Click Start, click Run, in the Open box, type **cmd**, and then press ENTER.

3. In the command prompt window, type **gpupdate**, and then press ENTER.

4. In the command prompt window, type **gpresult**, and then press ENTER.

5. In the Computer Settings section of the command window, the GPOs that were applied to the computer are displayed.

   Record the results in the space below:

   _____

   _____

   _____

6. Click Start, click Run, in the Open box, type **mmc**, and then press ENTER.

7. In the Console1 console, click the File menu from the menu bar, and then click Add/Remove Snap-In.

8. In the Add/Remove Snap-In window, click Add to open the Add Stand-Alone Snap-In window, click Resultant Set Of Policy, click Add, and then click Close to close the Add Standalone Snap-In window.

9. Click OK to close the Add/Remove Snap-In window.

10. In the Console1 console tree, right-click the Resultant Set Of Policy, and then click Generate RSoP Data to open the Resultant Set Of Policy Wizard.

11. On the Welcome To The Resultant Set Of Policy Wizard page, click Next.

12. In the Mode Selection page, verify that Logging Mode is selected, and then click Next to open the Computer Selection window.

13. On the Computer Selection page, verify that This Computer is selected, and then click Next to open the User Selection window.

14. On the User Selection page, click Next to open the Summary Of Selections page.

15. On the Summary Of Selections page, click Next.

16. On the Completing The Resultant Set Of Policy Wizard page, click Finish.

17. In the Console1 console tree, expand Administrator On Computer.*xx* RSoP (where Computer.*xx* is the name of your computer).

18. In the Console1 console tree, expand Computer Configuration\
Administrative Templates\Windows Components, and then select
Windows Update.

19. In the Console1 details pane, note the results and record them below:

Setting: _____

State: _____

GPO Name: _____

Configure Automatic Updates: _____

Specify intranet Microsoft Update service location: _____

Reschedule Automatic Updates scheduled installations: _____

No Auto-Restart For Scheduled Automatic Updates Installations:

_____

QUESTION   Are these the changes you made while creating and editing Group
Policy in the Configuring Software Update Services client options in the Group Policy
exercise you completed earlier in this Lab Manual?

QUESTION   What other GPOs are applied to the computer configuration? (Hint:
Right-click Computer Configuration, and then select Properties.)

20. Click Start, click Control Panel, and then click System to open the System
Properties window.

21. In the System Properties window, click the Automatic Updates tab.

QUESTION   Why do the settings appear dimmed in the Automatic Updates tab?
What does this tell you?

Verifying SUS Client Updates

IMPORTANT   Complete this task from the student computer with the higher number.
This will allow you to verify that the SUS client receives updates from the SUS server.

1. Start your computer running Windows Server 2003, and log on as
administrator@*domain*.contoso.com (where *domain* is the name of
your domain).

2. Click Start, and then click My Computer to open the My Computer window.

3. Navigate to the C:\Windows folder. Locate and then double-click the
Windows Update.log file to open it in Microsoft Notepad.

4. In the Windows Update.log Notepad window, locate *http://computerxx
/autoupdate/getmanifest.asp* (where *computerxx* is the name of your partner's
computer) to confirm that the Automatic Updates component is properly
redirecting to your SUS server.

EXERCISE 7-4: UNINSTALLING SUS

Estimated completion time: 10 minutes

In this exercise, you will remove Microsoft SUS that you installed and configured in the previous exercises. You will also remove the GPO settings. Completing these steps will remove any dependencies that might influence later lab exercises.

Removing Microsoft SUS

> **IMPORTANT** *Complete this task from the student computer with the lower number. This will allow you to uninstall SUS from a student computer.*

1. Start your computer running Windows Server 2003, and log on as **student*xx*@*domain*.contoso.com** (where student*xx* is your student User Name and *domain* is the name of your domain).

2. Click Start, and then click Control Panel.

3. While holding down the SHIFT key, right-click the Add Or Remove Programs option, and then click Run As to open the Run As dialog box.

4. In the Run As dialog box, select The Following User option, and then enter the following credentials in the dialog box fields to open the Add Or Remove Programs Wizard:

    a. In the User Name box, enter **administrator@*domain*.contoso.com** (where *domain* is the name of your domain).

    b. In the Password box, enter **MSPress@LS#1**.

5. Click OK to open the Add Or Remove Programs Wizard.

6. In the Add Or Remove Programs window, in the Currently Installed Programs section, click Microsoft Software Update Services, and then click Remove.

7. In the Add Or Remove Programs dialog box, click Yes to confirm the removal of SUS.

8. Close the Add Or Remove Programs window.

Removing Group Policy Settings

> **IMPORTANT** *Complete this task from the student computer with the lower number. This will allow you to delete the GPO that was created for configuring clients and servers on the network to use SUS.*

1. Start your computer running Windows Server 2003, and log on as **student*xx*@*domain*.contoso.com** (where student*xx* is your student User Name and *domain* is the name of your domain).

2. Click Start, click Control Panel, double-click Administrative Tools, right-click Active Directory Users And Computers, and then select Run As.

3. In the Run As dialog box, select The Following User option, and then enter the following credentials in the dialog box fields to open the Add Or Remove Programs Wizard:

    a. In the User Name box, enter **administrator@*domain*.contoso.com** (where *domain* is the name of your domain).

    b. In the Password box, enter **MSPress@LS#1**.

4. Click OK to open the Active Directory Users And Computers console.

5. In the Active Directory Users And Computers console, select and then right-click *Domain*.Contoso.Com (where *Domain* is the name of your domain), and then click Properties.

6. In the *Domain*.Contoso.Com Properties window, click the Group Policy tab.

7. In the Group Policy tab, in the Group Policy Object Links section, click Software Updates, and then click Delete.

8. In the Delete dialog box, click Remove The Link And Delete The Group Policy Object Permanently, and then click OK.

9. In the Delete Group Policy Object dialog box, click Yes to delete the GPO.

10. In the *Domain*.Contoso.Com Properties window, click Close.

11. Close the Active Directory Users And Computers console.

LAB REVIEW QUESTIONS

Estimated completion time: 15 minutes

1. Which port does SUS use to communicate with the Windows Update service?

2. Which Microsoft software products can be updated by using SUS?

3. Does SUS have the capability to update client and server service packs?

4. Which tools can you use to ensure that the SUS client receives the Group Policy settings?

5. If you have two SUS servers located on your network—one configured to update from the other—and they are both separated by a proxy server, how can you configure SUS to obtain updates?

6. Why is automatic approval of SUS updates for clients not a recommended practice?

7. After you install the SUS server, clients are unable to receive updates from the server. What are some possible reasons that the clients might not be able to receive updates?

8. Which file can be used to determine whether the SUS client receives updates from an internal SUS server?

9. What are two compelling reasons to use a chained SUS hierarchy to deliver updates to SUS clients on a network?

LAB CHALLENGE 7-1: CREATING A SUS HIERARCHY

Estimated completion time: 15 minutes

You are the security officer for Adventure Works (*http://www.adventure-works.com*). It has been brought to your attention that many of the client and server computers on the network have not been updated properly with security patches and service packs. Currently, you have one SUS computer running at the main office, but the performance of this server computer has been suffering because of the number of updates it sends to clients and servers on the network. It is connected to the Internet using a 512-kilobits per second (Kbps) digital subscriber line (DSL) connection. This connection is at 80 to 90 percent utilization.

You have two branch office locations that are connected to the main office with 256-Kbps DSL connections. These connections are at 75 to 80 percent utilization. Each branch office currently has approximately 200 to 250 client computers. You are concerned that even though you have Help Desk technicians on-site at each of the branch locations, many security updates are not being applied and the Help Desk technicians are not capable of managing a SUS server.

Devise a solution for deploying security updates and service packs to the client and server computers at the main and branch offices of your company network.

LAB 8
CONFIGURING ROUTING BY USING ROUTING AND REMOTE ACCESS

This lab contains the following exercises and activities:

- Exercise 8-1: Enabling Routing and Remote Access
- Exercise 8-2: Configuring IP Routing
- Exercise 8-3: Creating a VPN
- Exercise 8-4: Implementing Remote Access Policies
- Exercise 8-5: Configuring NAT
- Exercise 8-6: Configuring Packet Filters
- Exercise 8-7: Removing Routing and Remote Access
- Lab Review Questions
- Lab Challenge 8-1: Designing a Remote Access Solution

After completing this lab, you will be able to

- Install and configure Routing and Remote Access.
- Configure static and dynamic routing.
- Create a virtual private network (VPN).
- Use remote access policies to limit remote access connections.
- Configure Network Address Translation (NAT) to translate private Internet Protocol (IP) addresses.
- Create packet filters to limit IP traffic.

Estimated completion time: 145 minutes (This estimate includes the Before You Begin setup procedures.)

BEFORE YOU BEGIN

IMPORTANT   If you completed the exercises for Lab 5, "Network Security," and Lab 6, "Securing Network Traffic by Using IPSec," you are only required to complete one of the following prerequisite exercises, "Enabling and Configuring the Litware Inc Network Adapter."

To complete the exercises in Lab 8, you are required to install a second network adapter in each of the student computers. Connect the additional network adapters using crossover cables between them. After completing Lab 8, remove the second network adapters or disable them in the Microsoft Windows interface before continuing with the final Lab Manual lab exercises.

Estimated completion time: 10 minutes

Enabling and Configuring the Litware Inc Network Adapter

IMPORTANT   If you completed the exercises for Lab 5, "Network Security," and Lab 6, "Securing Network Traffic by Using IPSec," you are still required to complete the following prerequisite exercise, "Enabling and Configuring the Litware Inc Network Adapter."

1. Start your computer running Microsoft Windows Server 2003, and log on as **administrator@***domain*.**contoso.com** (where *domain* is the name of your domain).

2. Click Start, and then click Network Connections to open the Network Connections window.

3. In the Network Connections window, right-click the Litware Inc Network connection, and then click Enable.

4. In the Network Connections window, right-click the Litware Inc Network connection, and then click Properties to open the Litware Inc Network Properties page.

5. In the Litware Inc Network Properties page, click Internet Protocol (TCP/IP), and then click Properties.

6. In the General tab, select Use The Following IP Address, and enter the IP addressing information from Table 8-1.

Table 8-1   **Student Computer IP Addressing**

Computer Name	Contoso, Ltd., Network	Litware, Inc., Network
Computer01	IP address: 10.1.1.1 Subnet mask: 255.255.0.0	IP address: 192.168.0.1 Subnet mask: 255.255.255.0
Computer02	IP address: 10.1.1.2 Subnet mask: 255.255.0.0	IP address: 192.168.0.2 Subnet mask: 255.255.255.0
Computer03	IP address: 10.1.1.3 Subnet mask: 255.255.0.0	IP address: 192.168.0.3 Subnet mask: 255.255.255.0
Computer04	IP address: 10.1.1.4 Subnet mask: 255.255.0.0	IP address: 192.168.0.4 Subnet mask: 255.255.255.0
Computer05	IP address: 10.1.1.5 Subnet mask: 255.255.0.0	IP address: 192.168.0.5 Subnet mask: 255.255.255.0
Computer06	IP address: 10.1.1.6 Subnet mask: 255.255.0.0	IP address: 192.168.0.6 Subnet mask: 255.255.255.0

Table 8-1   **Student Computer IP Addressing**

Computer Name	Contoso, Ltd., Network	Litware, Inc., Network
Computer07	IP address: 10.1.1.7 Subnet mask: 255.255.0.0	IP address: 192.168.0.7 Subnet mask: 255.255.255.0
Computer08	IP address: 10.1.1.8 Subnet mask: 255.255.0.0	IP address: 192.168.0.8 Subnet mask: 255.255.255.0
Computer09	IP address: 10.1.1.9 Subnet mask: 255.255.0.0	IP address: 192.168.0.9 Subnet mask: 255.255.255.0
Computer10	IP address: 10.1.1.10 Subnet mask: 255.255.0.0	IP address: 192.168.0.10 Subnet mask: 255.255.255.0
Computer11	IP address: 10.1.1.11 Subnet mask: 255.255.0.0	IP address: 192.168.0.11 Subnet mask: 255.255.255.0
Computer12	IP address: 10.1.1.12 Subnet mask: 255.255.0.0	IP address: 192.168.0.12 Subnet mask: 255.255.255.0
Computer13	IP address: 10.1.1.13 Subnet mask: 255.255.0.0	IP address: 192.168.0.13 Subnet mask: 255.255.255.0
Computer14	IP address: 10.1.1.14 Subnet mask: 255.255.0.0	IP address: 192.168.0.14 Subnet mask: 255.255.255.0
Computer15	IP address: 10.1.1.15 Subnet mask: 255.255.0.0	IP address: 192.168.0.15 Subnet mask: 255.255.255.0
Computer16	IP address: 10.1.1.16 Subnet mask: 255.255.0.0	IP address: 192.168.0.16 Subnet mask: 255.255.255.0
Computer17	IP address: 10.1.1.17 Subnet mask: 255.255.0.0	IP address: 192.168.0.17 Subnet mask: 255.255.255.0
Computer18	IP address: 10.1.1.18 Subnet mask: 255.255.0.0	IP address: 192.168.0.18 Subnet mask: 255.255.255.0
Computer19	IP address: 10.1.1.19 Subnet mask: 255.255.0.0	IP address: 192.168.0.19 Subnet mask: 255.255.255.0
Computer20	IP address: 10.1.1.20 Subnet mask: 255.255.0.0	IP address: 192.168.0.20 Subnet mask: 255.255.255.0
Computer21	IP address: 10.1.1.21 Subnet mask: 255.255.0.0	IP address: 192.168.0.21 Subnet mask: 255.255.255.0
Computer22	IP address: 10.1.1.22 Subnet mask: 255.255.0.0	IP address: 192.168.0.22 Subnet mask: 255.255.255.0
Computer23	IP address: 10.1.1.23 Subnet mask: 255.255.0.0	IP address: 192.168.0.23 Subnet mask: 255.255.255.0
Computer24	IP address: 10.1.1.24 Subnet mask: 255.255.0.0	IP address: 192.168.0.24 Subnet mask: 255.255.255.0
Computer25	IP address: 10.1.1.25 Subnet mask: 255.255.0.0	IP address: 192.168.0.25 Subnet mask: 255.255.255.0
Computer26	IP address: 10.1.1.26 Subnet mask: 255.255.0.0	IP address: 192.168.0.26 Subnet mask: 255.255.255.0
Computer27	IP address: 10.1.1.27 Subnet mask: 255.255.0.0	IP address: 192.168.0.27 Subnet mask: 255.255.255.0
Computer28	IP address: 10.1.1.28 Subnet mask: 255.255.0.0	IP address: 192.168.0.28 Subnet mask: 255.255.255.0
Computer29	IP address: 10.1.1.29 Subnet mask: 255.255.0.0	IP address: 192.168.0.29 Subnet mask: 255.255.255.0
Computer30	IP address: 10.1.1.30 Subnet mask: 255.255.0.0	IP address: 192.168.0.30 Subnet mask: 255.255.255.0

7. After you enter the IP addressing information, click OK to close the Internet Protocol (TCP/IP) Properties window.

8. Click OK to close the Litware Inc Network Properties window.

9. Close the Network Connections window.

Installing the WWW Service

IMPORTANT   *Complete this task from both student computers. This will allow you to install the WWW service on your server that runs Windows Server 2003. You are only required to do this procedure if you didn't complete Lab 5 and Lab 6.*

1. Start your computer running Windows Server 2003, and log on as **studentxx@domain.contoso.com** (where studentxx is your student User Name and *domain* is the name of your domain).

2. Click Start, and then select Control Panel.

3. While holding down the SHIFT key, right-click Add Or Remove Programs, and then click Run As to open the Run As dialog box.

4. In the Run As dialog box, select The Following User option, and then enter the following credentials in the dialog box fields to open the Add Or Remove Programs window:

    a. In the User Name box, enter **administrator@ domain.contoso.com** (where *domain* is the name of your domain).

    b. In the Password box, enter **MSPress@LS#1**.

5. In the Add Or Remove Programs window, click Add/Remove Windows Components.

6. In the Components section in the Windows Components Wizard, select the Application Server option, and then click the Details button.

7. In the Application Server window, select Internet Information Services (IIS), and then click the Details button.

8. In the Internet Information Services (IIS) window, select the World Wide Web Service check box, and then click OK.

9. In the Internet Information Services (IIS) window, click OK.

10. In the Application Server window, click OK.

11. On the Windows Components page, click Next.

12. If asked for the location of the installation files, place the Windows Server 2003 installation CD into the CD-ROM drive, and then click OK.

13. On the Completing The Windows Components Wizard page, click Finish.

14. Close all open windows.

Configuring the WWW Service

IMPORTANT   *Complete this task from both student computers. This will allow you to configure the WWW service on your server that runs Windows Server 2003. You are only required to do this procedure if you didn't complete Lab 5 and Lab 6.*

1. Start your computer running Windows Server 2003, and log on as **administrator@*domain*.contoso.com** (where *domain* is the name of your domain).

2. Click Start, point to All Programs, select Accessories, and then click Notepad to open Microsoft Notepad.

3. In the Untitled—Notepad window, type the following text:

```
<html>
<head>
<title>Welcome to the World Wide Web</title>
</head>
<body>
<p><font color="#0066CC"
face="Arial"><b>This is the default page for the World
Wide Web service!!</b></font></p>
</body>
</html>
```

4. In the Untitled—Notepad window, click File, and then click Save As.

5. In the Save As window, click My Computer on the left, and then navigate to the C:\Inetpub\Wwwroot folder.

6. In the Save As window, type **default.htm** in the File Name box, and then click Save to save the Default.htm file to the C:\Inetpub\Wwwroot folder.

7. Close Notepad.

Increasing the Domain Functional Level

IMPORTANT   *Complete this task from the student computer that has the lower number. This will allow you to implement Routing and Remote Access policies. You are only required to do this procedure if you didn't complete Lab 5 and Lab 6.*

1. Start your computer running Windows Server 2003, and log on as **student*xx*@*domain*.contoso.com** (where student*xx* is your student User Name and *domain* is the name of your domain).

2. Click Start, select Control Panel, and then double-click Administrative Tools.

3. Right-click Active Directory Users And Computers, and then click Run As to open the Run As dialog box.

4. Select The Following User option, and then enter the following credentials in the dialog box fields:

    a. In the User Name box, enter **administrator@*domain*.contoso.com** (where *domain* is the name of your domain).

    b. In the Password box, enter **MSPress@LS#1**.

5. Right-click *Domain*.Contoso.Com (where *Domain* is the name of your domain), and then click Raise Domain Functional Level to open the Raise Domain Functional Level window.

6. In the Raise Domain Functional Level window, select Windows Server 2003 from the Select An Available Domain Functional Level option.

7. Click the Raise button to raise the domain functional level.

8. Click OK to accept the Raise Domain Functional Level warning box.

9. Click OK to accept the Raise Domain Functional Level information dialog box.

SCENARIO

You are the network administrator for Contoso, Ltd. Recently, your company has purchased a new company named Litware, Inc. Contoso, Ltd.'s main office is located in an office building in Denver. Litware, Inc.'s main office is located across the city. The Litware, Inc., network only contains 8 to 10 users that are connected to the Contoso, Ltd., network via a 56 Frame Relay connection. In order to connect the two main office networks you need to install and configure Routing and Remote Access on a Microsoft Windows Server 2003 server in both locations. This will allow users on both networks to access resources on both networks and also provide remote access for clients.

EXERCISE 8-1: ENABLING ROUTING AND REMOTE ACCESS

Estimated completion time: 5 minutes

You are the network administrator for Contoso, Ltd. Before you can get the two networks to communicate, you must first install Routing and Remote Access.

Installing Routing and Remote Access

IMPORTANT   Complete this task from both student computers. This will allow you to install Routing and Remote Access on your student computer.

1. Start your computer running Windows Server 2003, and log on as **student*xx*@*domain*.contoso.com** (where student*xx* is your student User Name and *domain* is the name of your domain).

2. Click Start, select Control Panel, and then double-click Administrative Tools.

3. Right-click Routing And Remote Access, and then select Run As to open the Run As dialog box.

4. In the Run As dialog box, select The Following User option, and then enter the following credentials in the dialog box fields to open the Routing And Remote Access console:

   a. In the User Name box, enter **administrator@*domain*.contoso.com** (where *domain* is the name of your domain).

   b. In the Password box, enter **MSPress@LS#1**.

5. Click OK to open the Routing And Remote Access console.

6. In the Routing And Remote Access console tree, right-click Computer*xx* (where Computer*xx* is the name of your computer), and then select Configure And Enable Routing And Remote Access from the shortcut menu.

7. On the Welcome To Routing And Remote Access Server Setup Wizard page, click Next to open the Configuration page.

8. On the Configuration page, click Custom Configuration, and then click Next to open the Custom Configuration page.

9. On the Custom Configuration page, click LAN Routing, and then click Next to open the Completing The Routing And Remote Access Server Setup Wizard.

10. On the Completing The Routing And Remote Access Server Setup Wizard page, click Finish to close the Routing And Remote Access Server Setup Wizard.

11. In the Routing And Remote Access dialog box, click Yes to start the Routing and Remote Access service.

12. Close the Routing And Remote Access console.

EXERCISE 8-2: CONFIGURING IP ROUTING

Estimated completion time: 15 minutes

To connect the Litware and Contoso networks, you must configure both Routing and Remote Access servers to contain the proper routes for both networks in their routing tables. You must now add the Routing Information Protocol (RIP) to both Routing and Remote Access servers to enable communication between the two networks.

Installing and Configuring RIP

IMPORTANT *Complete this task from both student computers. This will allow you to configure your Routing and Remote Access server as a RIP router.*

1. Start your computer running Windows Server 2003, and log on as **student*xx*@*domain*.contoso.com** (where student*xx* is your student User Name and *domain* is the name of your domain).

2. Click Start, select Control Panel, and then double-click Administrative Tools.

3. Right-click Routing And Remote Access, and then select Run As to open the Run As dialog box.

4. In the Run As dialog box, select The Following User option, and then enter the following credentials in the dialog box fields to open the Routing And Remote Access console:

    a. In the User Name box, enter **administrator@*domain*.contoso.com** (where *domain* is the name of your domain).

    b. In the Password box, enter **MSPress@LS#1**.

5. Click OK to open the Routing And Remote Access console.

6. In the Routing And Remote Access console tree, expand Computer.*xx* (where Computer.*xx* is the name of your computer), and then expand IP Routing.

7. Under IP Routing, select and right-click General, and then select New Routing Protocol.

8. On the New Routing Protocol page, click RIP Version 2 For Internet Protocol, and then click OK.

9. In the Routing And Remote Access window, right-click RIP, and then select New Interface.

10. In the New Interface For RIP Version 2 For Internet Protocol window, under Interfaces, choose Contoso Ltd Network, and click OK.

11. On the RIP Properties—Contoso Ltd Network Properties page, click OK.

12. In the Routing And Remote Access window, right-click RIP, and then select New Interface.

13. In the New Interface For RIP Version 2 For Internet Protocol window, under Interfaces, choose Litware Inc Network, and then click OK.

14. On the RIP Properties—Litware Inc Network Properties page, click OK.

Verifying RIP Neighbors

IMPORTANT   *Complete this task on both student computers. This will allow you to view RIP neighbors. These are other RIP routers to which this RIP router communicates routing information.*

1. Start your computer running Windows Server 2003, and log on as **student*xx*@*domain*.contoso.com** (where student.*xx* is your student User Name and *domain* is the name of your domain).

2. Click Start, select Control Panel, and then double-click Administrative Tools.

3. Right-click Routing And Remote Access, and then select Run As to open the Run As dialog box.

4. In the Run As dialog box, select The Following User option, and then enter the following credentials in the dialog box fields to open the Routing And Remote Access console:

    a. In the User Name box, enter **administrator@*domain*.contoso.com** (where *domain* is the name of your domain).

    b. In the Password box, enter **MSPress@LS#1**.

5. Click OK to open the Routing And Remote Access console.

6. In the Routing And Remote Access console tree, expand Computer.*xx* (where Computer.*xx* is the name of your computer), and then expand IP Routing.

7. In the Routing And Remote Access console tree, right-click RIP, and then select Show Neighbors.

   QUESTION   Is the IP address of your partner's computer listed in the Computerxx - RIP Neighbors window?

8. Close the Routing And Remote Access console.

Adding Static Routes

IMPORTANT   Complete this task from both student computers. This will allow you to add static routes to your server that runs Windows Server 2003.

1. Start your computer running Windows Server 2003, and log on as **studentxx@domain.contoso.com** (where studentxx is your student User Name and *domain* is the name of your domain).

2. Click Start, select Control Panel, and then double-click Administrative Tools.

3. Right-click Routing And Remote Access, and then select Run As to open the Run As dialog box.

4. In the Run As dialog box, select The Following User option, and then enter the following credentials in the dialog box fields to open the Routing And Remote Access console:

   a. In the User Name box, enter **administrator@domain.contoso.com** (where *domain* is the name of your domain).

   b. In the Password box, enter **MSPress@LS#1**.

5. Click OK to open the Routing And Remote Access console.

6. In the Routing And Remote Access console tree, expand Computerxx (where Computerxx is the name of your computer), and then expand IP Routing.

7. In the Routing And Remote Access console tree, right-click Static Routes, and then click New Static Route to open the Static Route window.

8. In the Static Route Interface field drop-down list, select the Litware Inc Network adapter.

9. In the Static Route Destination box, type **172.16.0.0**.

10. In the Static Route Network Mask box, type **255.255.255.0**.

11. In the Static Route Gateway box, type the IP address of your Litware Inc Network adapter.

12. Click OK in the Static Route window.

Verifying Static Routes Using the Routing And Remote Access Console

IMPORTANT   *Complete this task from both student computers. This will allow you to view and verify that the static routes were added to your server that runs Windows Server 2003.*

1. Start your computer running Windows Server 2003, and log on as **student*xx*@*domain*.contoso.com** (where student*xx* is your student User Name and *domain* is the name of your domain).

2. Click Start, select Control Panel, and then double-click Administrative Tools.

3. Right-click Routing And Remote Access, and then select Run As to open the Run As dialog box.

4. In the Run As dialog box, select The Following User option, and then enter the following credentials in the dialog box fields to open the Routing And Remote Access console:

   a. In the User Name box, enter **administrator@*domain*.contoso.com** (where *domain* is the name of your domain).

   b. In the Password box, enter **MSPress@LS#1**.

5. Click OK to open the Routing And Remote Access console.

6. In the Routing And Remote Access console tree, expand Computer*xx* (where Computer*xx* is the name of your computer), and then expand IP Routing.

7. In the Routing And Remote Access console tree, right-click Static Routes, and then select Show IP Routing Table.

   Record the route information for the 172.16.0.0 network in the following table:

Route Information	Route 1	Route 2
Destination		
Network Mask		
Gateway		
Interface		
Metric		
Protocol		

QUESTION   *Is this the static route you added in the previous steps?*

Verifying Static Routes Using the Routing And Remote Access Console

IMPORTANT Complete this task from both student computers. This will allow you to view and verify that the static routes were added to your server that runs Windows Server 2003.

1. Start your computer running Windows Server 2003, and log on as **studentxx@domain.contoso.com** (where studentxx is your student User Name and *domain* is the name of your domain).

2. Click Start, click Run, type **cmd** in the Open box, and then press ENTER.

3. In the command prompt window, at the command prompt, type **route print**.

   QUESTION Is there a static route for the 172.16.0.0 network that you added in the previous steps?

4. Close the command prompt window.

Deleting Static Routes

IMPORTANT Complete this task from both student computers. This will allow you to delete the static routes that were added to your server that runs Windows Server 2003.

1. Start your computer running Windows Server 2003, and log on as **studentxx@domain.contoso.com** (where studentxx is your student User Name and *domain* is the name of your domain).

2. Click Start, select Control Panel, and then double-click Administrative Tools.

3. Right-click Routing And Remote Access, and then select Run As to open the Run As dialog box.

4. In the Run As dialog box, select The Following User option, and then enter the following credentials in the dialog box fields to open the Routing And Remote Access console:

   a. In the User Name box, enter **administrator@domain.contoso.com** (where *domain* is the name of your domain).

   b. In the Password box, enter **MSPress@LS#1**.

5. Click OK to open the Routing And Remote Access console.

6. In the Routing And Remote Access console tree, expand Computerxx, and then expand IP Routing.

7. In the Routing And Remote Access console tree, click Static Routes.

8. In the details pane of the Routing And Remote Access console, right-click the static route 172.16.0.0, and then click Delete.

9. Close the Routing And Remote Access console.

EXERCISE 8-3: CREATING A VPN

Estimated completion time: 20 minutes

There are several Finance department employees that must securely transfer financial and accounting data from the Litware network to the Contoso network. You must create a secure VPN connection for those client computers so that the users can securely transfer the financial data to a server on the Contoso network.

Configuring a VPN Server

IMPORTANT Complete this task from the student computer with the lower number. This will allow you to configure Routing and Remote Access with VPN ports.

1. Start your computer running Windows Server 2003, and log on as **studentxx@domain.contoso.com** (where studentxx is your student User Name and *domain* is the name of your domain).

2. Click Start, select Control Panel, and then double-click Administrative Tools.

3. Right-click Routing And Remote Access, and then select Run As to open the Run As dialog box.

4. In the Run As dialog box, select The Following User option, and then enter the following credentials in the dialog box fields to open the Routing And Remote Access console:

   a. In the User Name box, enter **administrator@domain.contoso.com** (where *domain* is the name of your domain).

   b. In the Password box, enter **MSPress@LS#1**.

5. Click OK to open the Routing And Remote Access console.

6. In the Routing And Remote Access console tree, right-click Computerxx (where Computerxx is the name of your computer), and then click Properties to open the Computerxx (Local) Properties page.

7. On the Computerxx (Local) Properties page, in the General tab, select the Remote Access Server check box, and then click OK.

8. In the Routing And Remote Access dialog box, click Yes to restart the router.

   QUESTION How many default VPN ports are enabled after you configured Routing and Remote Access?

   QUESTION How can you configure more VPN ports?

9. Close all open windows.

Adding a VPN User Account

IMPORTANT   *Complete this task from the student computer with the lower number. This will allow you to create a user account that will be used to establish a VPN
connection with the VPN server.*

1. Start your computer running Windows Server 2003, and log on as
   studentxx@domain.contoso.com (where studentxx is your student
   User Name and *domain* is the name of your domain).

2. Click Start, select Control Panel, and then double-click Administrative
   Tools.

3. Right-click Active Directory Users And Computers, and then select Run As
   to open the Run As dialog box.

4. In the Run As dialog box, select The Following User option, and then
   enter the following credentials in the dialog box fields to open the Active
   Directory Users And Computers console:

   a. In the User Name box, enter **administrator@domain.contoso.com**
      (where *domain* is the name of your domain).

   b. In the Password box, enter **MSPress@LS#1**.

5. Click OK to open the Active Directory Users And Computers console.

6. In the Active Directory Users And Computers console tree, right-click
   Domain.Contoso.Com (where *Domain* is the name of your domain),
   select New, and then click Organizational Unit.

7. In the New Object—Organizational Unit window, in the Name box, type
   vpn users, and then click OK.

8. In the Active Directory Users And Computers console tree, right-click the
   VPN Users organizational unit (OU), click New, and then click User to
   open the New Object—User window.

9. In the New Object—User window, in the First Name box, type **VPNUser**.

10. In the New Object—User window, in the User Logon Name box, type
    VPNUser, and then click Next.

11. In the Password and Confirm Password boxes, type **MSPress#1**, clear the
    User Must Change Password At Next Logon option, select the User Can-
    not Change Password option, and then click Next.

12. In the New Object—User window, click Finish to finish creating the new
    user account.

13. Close all open windows.

Connecting to a VPN Client

IMPORTANT   *Complete this task from the student computer with the higher number. This will allow you to attempt to connect to a VPN server.*

1. Start your computer running Windows Server 2003, and log on as **administrator@*domain*.contoso.com** (where *domain* is the name of your domain).

2. Click Start, and click Network Connections to open the Network Connections window.

3. In the Network Connections window, on the file menu, click New Connection to open the New Connection Wizard.

4. In the New Connection Wizard, click Next to open the Network Connection Type page.

5. In the Network Connection Type page, click Connect To The Network At My Workplace, and then click Next.

6. On the Network Connection page, click Virtual Private Network connection, and then click Next to open the Connection Name page.

7. On the Connection Name page, in the Company Name box, type **vpn to contoso ltd**, and then click Next.

8. On the VPN Server Selection page, in the Host Name Or IP Address field, type the IP address of your partner's computer (10.1.1.*x*), and then click Next.

9. On the Connection Availability page, select Anyone's Use, and then click Next.

10. On the Completing the New Connection Wizard page, select the Add A Shortcut To This Connection To My Desktop check box, and then click Finish to close the New Connection Wizard.

11. In the Connect VPN To Contoso Ltd window, type the following credentials:

    a. In the User Name box, enter **VPNUser**.

    b. In the Password box, enter **MSPress#1**.

12. Click Connect to connect the VPN connection.

    QUESTION   *Which error message appears when you try to connect to the VPN server?*

13. On the Error Connecting To VPN To Contoso Ltd page, click Close.

Configuring a VPN User Account

IMPORTANT *Complete this task from the student computer with the lower number. This will allow you to configure the dial-in permissions for a user account.*

1. Start your computer running Windows Server 2003, and log on as **student*xx*@*domain*.contoso.com** (where student*xx* is your student User Name and *domain* is the name of your domain).

2. Click Start, click Control Panel, and then double-click Administrative Tools.

3. Right-click Active Directory Users And Computers, and then select Run As to open the Run As dialog box.

4. In the Run As dialog box, select The Following User option, and then enter the following credentials in the dialog box fields to open the Active Directory Users And Computers console:

    a. In the User Name box, enter **administrator@*domain*.contoso.com** (where *domain* is the name of your domain).

    b. In the Password box, enter **MSPress@LS#1**.

5. Click OK to open the Active Directory Users And Computers console.

6. In the Active Directory Users And Computers console tree, expand *Domain*.Contoso.Com (where *Domain* is the name of your domain), and then select VPN Users.

7. In the details pane of the Active Directory Users And Computers console, right-click VPNUser, and then click Properties.

8. On the VPNUser Properties page, click the Dial-In tab, click Allow Access, and then click OK.

    QUESTION *Which dial-in option is enabled by default?*

9. Close all open windows.

Reconnecting to a VPN Client

IMPORTANT *Complete this task from the student computer with the higher number. This will allow you to attempt to make a connection to a VPN server.*

1. Start your computer running Windows Server 2003, and log on as **student*xx*@*domain*.contoso.com** (where student*xx* is your student User Name and *domain* is the name of your domain).

2. On the desktop, double-click the VPN To Contoso Ltd dial-up connection icon.

3. In the Connect VPN To Contoso Ltd window, type the following credentials:

    a. In the User Name box, enter **VPNUser**.

    b. In the Password box, enter **MSPress#1**.

4. Click Connect to connect to the VPN connection.

> **QUESTION**   Which error message do you receive when you try to connect to the VPN server?

5. On the Error Connecting To VPN To Contoso Ltd page, click Close.

> **QUESTION**   Why was the VPNUser not allowed to connect with the Control Access Through Remote Access Policy dial-in option enabled for the VPNUser account?

Reconfiguring a VPN Server

> **IMPORTANT**   Complete this task from the student computer with the lower number. This will allow you to accept inbound VPN connections.

1. Start your computer running Windows Server 2003, and log on as **student*xx*@*domain*.contoso.com** (where student*xx* is your student User Name and *domain* is the name of your domain).

2. Click Start, select Control Panel, and then double-click Administrative Tools.

3. Right-click Routing And Remote Access, and select Run As to open the Run As dialog box.

4. In the Run As dialog box, select The Following User option, and then enter the following credentials in the dialog box fields to open the Routing And Remote Access console:

    a. In the User Name box, enter **administrator@*domain*.contoso.com** (where *domain* is the name of your domain).

    b. In the Password box, enter **MSPress@LS#1**.

5. Click OK to open the Routing And Remote Access console.

6. In the Routing And Remote Access console tree, expand Computer*xx* (where Computer*xx* is the name of your computer).

7. In the Routing And Remote Access console tree, right-click Ports, and then select Properties.

8. In the Ports Properties window, select WAN Miniport (PPTP), and then click Configure.

9. On the Configure Device—WAN Miniport (PPTP) window, check the Remote Access Connections (Inbound Only) check box, and then click OK.

10. In the Ports Properties window, select WAN Miniport (L2TP), and then click Configure.

11. In the Configure Device—WAN Miniport (L2TP) window, select the Remote Access Connections (Inbound Only) check box, and then click OK.

12. In the Ports Properties window, click OK to accept your changes.

13. Close all open windows.

Reconnecting to a VPN Client

IMPORTANT Complete this task from the student computer with the higher number. This will allow you to connect to a VPN server.

1. Start your computer running Windows Server 2003, and log on as **student*xx*@*domain*.contoso.com** (where student*xx* is your student User Name and *domain* is the name of your domain).

2. On the desktop, double-click the VPN To Contoso Ltd dial-up connection icon.

3. In the Connect VPN To Contoso Ltd window, type the following credentials:

    a. In the User Name box, enter **VPNUser**.

    b. In the Password box, enter **MSPress#1**.

4. Click Connect to connect the VPN connection to Contoso Ltd.

5. A network connection icon appears in the notification area.

QUESTION Which VPN protocol and encryption method are used by this VPN connection? (Hint: Double-click the Network Connection icon on the taskbar.)

6. Close the VPN To Contoso Ltd Status window.

Viewing the Remote Access Connection

IMPORTANT Complete this task from the student computer with the lower number. This will allow you to view a VPN connection.

1. Start your computer running Windows Server 2003, and log on as **student*xx*@*domain*.contoso.com** (where student*xx* is your student User Name and *domain* is the name of your domain).

2. Click Start, select Control Panel, and then double-click Administrative Tools.

3. Right-click Routing And Remote Access, and then select Run As to open the Run As dialog box.

4. In the Run As dialog box, select The Following User option, and then enter the following credentials in the dialog box fields to open the Routing And Remote Access console:

   a. In the User Name box, enter **administrator@*domain*.contoso.com** (where *domain* is the name of your domain).

   b. In the Password box, enter **MSPress@LS#1**.

5. Click OK to open the Routing And Remote Access console.

6. In the Routing And Remote Access console tree, expand Computer*xx* (where Computer*xx* is the name of your computer), and then click Remote Access Clients.

   QUESTION   In the details pane of the Routing And Remote Access console, what is the name of the user who is currently connected?

Disconnecting the Remote Access Connection

IMPORTANT   Complete this task from the student computer with the higher number. This will allow you to disconnect from a VPN server.

1. Right-click the Network Connection icon for VPN To Contoso Ltd, and click Disconnect.

2. Close all open windows.

EXERCISE 8-4: IMPLEMENTING REMOTE ACCESS POLICIES

Estimated completion time: 25 minutes

You are the security administrator for Litware, Inc. Several of the users in the Finance department need remote VPN access to the remote access server at Contoso's main office. You must control user access to the VPN server beyond simply allowing users to connect to it. You must limit the types of remote access connections to the server to PPTP connections only. You want to implement remote access policies on the VPN server to control the specific user and connection properties.

Configuring a User Account Dial-In Properties

IMPORTANT   Complete this task from the student computer with the lower number. This will allow you to configure the dial-in permissions for a user account.

1. Start your computer running Windows Server 2003, and log on as **student*xx*@*domain*.contoso.com** (where student*xx* is your student User Name and *domain* is the name of your domain).

2. Click Start, select Control Panel, and then double-click Administrative Tools.

3. Right-click Active Directory Users And Computers, and then select Run As to open the Run As dialog box.

4. In the Run As dialog box, select The Following User option, and then enter the following credentials in the dialog box fields to open the Active Directory Users And Computers console:

   a. In the User Name box, enter **administrator@*domain*.contoso.com** (where *domain* is the name of your domain).

   b. In the Password box, enter **MSPress@LS#1**.

5. Click OK to open the Active Directory Users And Computers console.

6. In the Active Directory Users And Computers console tree, expand *Domain*.Contoso.Com (where *Domain* is the name of your domain), and then select VPN Users.

7. In the details pane of the Active Directory Users And Computers console, right-click VPNUser, and then click Properties.

8. On the VPNUser Properties page, click the Dial-In tab, select the Control Access Through Remote Access Policy option, and then click OK.

9. Close the Active Directory Users And Computers console.

   QUESTION   By changing the user account in this way, will the user be able to connect to the remote access server?

Testing the Default Remote Access Policy

IMPORTANT   Complete this task from the student computer with the higher number. This will allow you to test the default remote access policy on the Routing and Remote Access server.

1. Start your computer running Windows Server 2003, and log on as **student*xx*@*domain*.contoso.com** (where student*xx* is your student User Name and *domain* is the name of your domain).

2. On the desktop, double-click the VPN To Contoso Ltd dial-up connection icon.

3. In the Connect VPN To Contoso Ltd window, type the following credentials:

   a. In the User Name box, enter **VPNUser**.

   b. In the Password box, enter **MSPress#1**.

   c. In the Domain field, enter **_domain_.contoso.com** (where *domain* is the name of your domain).

4. Click Connect to connect the VPN connection to Contoso Ltd.

   QUESTION   Which error message did you receive?

5. Close the Error Connecting To VPN To Contoso Ltd window.

Configuring Remote Access Policy Conditions

IMPORTANT   Complete this task from the student computer with the lower number. This will allow you to configure the Routing and Remote Access server to accept only PPTP VPN connections.

1. Start your computer running Windows Server 2003, and log on as **studentxx@domain.contoso.com** (where studentxx is your student User Name and *domain* is the name of your domain).

2. Click Start, select Control Panel, and then double-click Administrative Tools.

3. Right-click Routing And Remote Access, and select Run As to open the Run As dialog box.

4. In the Run As dialog box, select The Following User option, and then enter the following credentials in the dialog box fields to open the Routing And Remote Access console:

   a. In the User Name box, enter **administrator@domain.contoso.com** (where *domain* is the name of your domain).

   b. In the Password box, enter **MSPress@LS#1**.

5. Click OK to open the Routing And Remote Access console.

6. In the Routing And Remote Access console tree, expand Computerxx (where Computerxx is the name of your computer).

7. Select and right-click Remote Access Policies, and then select New Remote Access Policy to open the New Remote Access Policy Wizard.

8. On the Welcome To The New Remote Access Policy Wizard page, click Next to open the Policy Configuration Method page.

9. On the Policy Configuration Method page, click Set Up A Custom Policy. In the Policy Name box, type **pptp only connections**, and then click Next.

10. On the Policy Conditions page, click Add to open the Select Attribute page.

11. On the Select Attribute page, click Tunnel-Type, and then click Add to open the Tunnel-Type page.

12. On the Tunnel-Type page, click Point-To-Point Tunneling Protocol (PPTP), under Selected Types, click Add to add Point-To-Point Tunneling Protocol (PPTP) to the list, and then click OK.

13. On the Policy Conditions page, click Next to open the Permissions page.

14. On the Permissions page, click Grant Remote Access Permission, and then click Next.

15. On the Profile page, click Next to open the Completing The New Remote Access Policy Wizard page.

16. On the Completing The New Remote Access Policy Wizard page, click Finish to close the New Remote Access Policy Wizard.

17. Close the Routing And Remote Access console.

Testing the Remote Access Policy Conditions

IMPORTANT   Complete this task from the student computer with the higher number. This will allow you to test the remote access policy that has been configured on the Routing and Remote Access server.

1. Start your computer running Windows Server 2003, and log on as **administrator@*domain*.contoso.com** (where *domain* is the name of your domain).

2. On the desktop, double-click the VPN To Contoso Ltd dial-up connection icon.

3. In the Connect VPN To Contoso Ltd window, type the following credentials:

 a. In the User Name box, enter **VPNUser**.

 b. In the Password box, enter **MSPress#1**.

4. Click Connect to connect the VPN connection to Contoso Ltd.

QUESTION   Does the VPN connection connect to the remote access server?

5. Right-click the VPN To Contoso Ltd icon on the desktop, and then select Disconnect.

6. Double-click the VPN To Contoso Ltd icon on the desktop, and then in the Connect VPN To Contoso Ltd window, click Properties.

7. On the VPN To Contoso Ltd Properties page, click the Networking tab, and in the Type Of VPN drop-down list, select L2TP IPSec VPN, and then click OK.

8. In the Connect VPN To Contoso Ltd window, type the following credentials:

 a. In the User Name box, enter **VPNUser**.

 b. In the Password box, enter **MSPress#1**.

QUESTION   Does the VPN connection connect to the remote access server? Why or why not?

9. Close the Error Connecting To VPN To Contoso Ltd window.

10. Double-click the VPN To Contoso Ltd icon on the desktop, and then, in the Connect VPN To Contoso Ltd window, click Properties.

11. On the VPN To Contoso Ltd Properties page, click the Networking tab, and in the Type Of VPN drop-down list, select PPTP VPN, and then click OK.

12. Click Cancel to close the Connect VPN To Contoso Ltd window.

Configuring Remote Access Policy Profile

IMPORTANT   Complete this task from the student computer with the lower number. This will allow you to configure the Routing and Remote Access server to accept only PPTP VPN connections for a given time period.

1. Start your computer running Windows Server 2003, and log on as **studentxx@domain.contoso.com** (where studentxx is your student User Name and *domain* is the name of your domain).

2. Click Start, select Control Panel, and then double-click Administrative Tools.

3. Right-click Routing And Remote Access, and then select Run As to open the Run As dialog box.

4. In the Run As dialog box, select The Following User option, and then enter the following credentials in the dialog box fields to open the Routing And Remote Access console:

   a. In the User Name box, enter **administrator@domain.contoso.com** (where *domain* is the name of your domain).

   b. In the Password box, enter **MSPress@LS#1**.

5. Click OK to open the Routing And Remote Access console.

6. In the Routing And Remote Access console tree, expand Computerxx (where Computerxx is the name of your computer).

7. Select Remote Access Policies, and in the details pane, right-click the PPTP Only Connections Remote Access policy, and then select Properties.

8. On the PPTP Only Connections Properties page, click Edit Profile to open the Edit Dial-In Profile window.

9. On the Edit Dial-In Profile window, select the Allow Access Only On These Days And At These Times check box, and then click Edit to open the Dial-In Hours window.

10. On the Dial-In Hours window, permit connections from only 6:00 A.M. to 7:00 A.M., and then click OK.

11. On the Edit Dial-In Profile page, click OK.

12. On the PPTP Only Connections Properties page, click OK.

13. Close the Routing And Remote Access console.

IMPORTANT   Notice the hours listed in the Allow Access Only On These Days And At These Times box change to Sunday–Saturday and 6:00 A.M. to 7:00 A.M., respectively.

Testing the Remote Access Policy Profile

IMPORTANT *Complete this task from the student computer with the higher number. This will allow you to test the remote access policy profile that has been configured on the Routing and Remote Access server.*

1. Start your computer running Windows Server 2003, and log on as **student*xx*@*domain*.contoso.com** (where student*xx* is your student User Name and *domain* is the name of your domain).

2. On the desktop, double-click the VPN To Contoso Ltd dial-up connection icon.

3. In the Connect VPN To Contoso Ltd window, type the following credentials:

   a. In the User Name box, enter **VPNUser**.

   b. In the Password box, enter **MSPress#1**.

4. Click Connect to connect the VPN connection to Contoso Ltd.

   QUESTION *Which error message did you receive and why?*

5. Close the Error Connecting To VPN To Contoso Ltd window.

Reconfiguring Remote Access Policy Profile

IMPORTANT *Complete this task from the student computer with the lower number. This will allow you to reconfigure the Routing and Remote Access server to accept only PPTP VPN connections.*

1. Start your computer running Windows Server 2003, and log on as **student*xx*@*domain*.contoso.com** (where student*xx* is your student User Name and *domain* is the name of your domain).

2. Click Start, select Control Panel, and then double-click Administrative Tools.

3. Right-click Routing And Remote Access, and select Run As to open the Run As dialog box.

4. In the Run As dialog box, select The Following User option, and then enter the following credentials in the dialog box fields to open the Routing And Remote Access console:

   a. In the User Name box, enter **administrator@*domain*.contoso.com** (where *domain* is the name of your domain).

   b. In the Password box, enter **MSPress#1**.

5. Click OK to open the Routing And Remote Access console.

6. In the Routing And Remote Access console tree, expand Computer.*xx* (where Computer.*xx* is the name of your computer).

7. Locate and select Remote Access Policies, in the Details pane, right-click the PPTP Only Connections Remote Access policy, and then select Properties.

8. On the PPTP Only Connections Properties page, click Edit Profile to open the Edit Dial-In Profile window.

9. In the Edit Dial-In Profile window, clear the Allow Access Only On These Days And At These Times option, and then click OK.

10. On the PPTP Only Connections Properties page, click OK.

11. Close all open windows.

Retesting the Remote Access Policy Profile

IMPORTANT   Complete this task from the student computer with the higher number. This will allow you to retest the remote access policy profile that has been configured on the Routing and Remote Access server.

1. Start your computer running Windows Server 2003, and log on as **student*xx*@*domain*.contoso.com** (where student*xx* is your student User Name and *domain* is the name of your domain).

2. On the desktop, double-click the VPN To Contoso Ltd dial-up connection icon.

3. In the Connect VPN To Contoso Ltd window, type the following credentials:

   a. In the User Name box, enter **VPNUser**.

   b. In the Password box, enter **MSPress#1**.

4. Click Connect to connect the VPN connection to Contoso Ltd.

   QUESTION   Were you allowed to connect to the remote access server? Why or why not?

5. Disconnect the VPN To Contoso Ltd connection.

EXERCISE 8-5: CONFIGURING NAT

Estimated completion time: 15 minutes

IMPORTANT   For the purpose of this exercise, assume that your student domain will be the equivalent of the Litware, Inc., network, and the classroom network will be the equivalent of the Contoso, Ltd., network. The student computer with the lower number will act as the NAT server, and the student computer with the higher number will act as a NAT client.

You are in the process of deploying NAT as the means for clients to connect to the Contoso network. You now must configure Routing and Remote Access with NAT and two different network interfaces to allow client connectivity.

Installing and Configuring NAT

IMPORTANT *Complete this task from the student computer with the lower number. This will allow you to install and configure NAT on your server that runs Windows Server 2003.*

1. Start your computer running Windows Server 2003, and log on as **student*xx*@*domain*.contoso.com** (where student*xx* is your student User Name and *domain* is the name of your domain).

2. Click Start, select Control Panel, and then double-click Administrative Tools.

3. Right-click Routing And Remote Access, and then select Run As to open the Run As dialog box.

4. In the Run As dialog box, select The Following User option, and then enter the following credentials in the dialog box fields to open the Routing And Remote Access console:

    a. In the User Name box, enter **administrator@*domain*.contoso.com** (where *domain* is the name of your domain).

    b. In the Password box, enter **MSPress@LS#1**.

5. Click OK to open the Routing And Remote Access console.

6. In the Routing And Remote Access console tree, expand Computer*xx* (where Computer*xx* is the name of your computer), and then expand IP Routing.

7. In the Routing And Remote Access console tree, select and right-click NAT/Basic Firewall, and then select New Interface.

8. In the New Interface For Network Address Translation (NAT) window, click the Contoso Ltd Network network adapter, and then click OK.

9. On the Network Address Translation (NAT) Properties—Contoso Ltd Network page, click Public Interface Connected To The Internet, select the Enable NAT On This Interface check box, and then click OK.

10. In the Routing And Remote Access console tree, right-click NAT/Basic Firewall, and then select New Interface.

11. In the New Interface For Network Address Translation (NAT) window, click the Litware Inc Network connection, and then click OK.

12. On the Network Address Translation (NAT) Properties—Litware Inc Network page, verify that the Private Interface Connected To Private Network option is selected, and then click OK.

13. Close all open windows.

Configuring a NAT Client

IMPORTANT   *For the remainder of this exercise, remove the network cable from the Contoso Ltd Network adapter on the higher numbered computer. At the end of Exercise 8-5, reconnect the network cable to the Contoso Ltd Network adapter on the NAT client. Complete this task from the student computer with the higher number. This will allow you to configure your computer as a NAT client.*

1. Start your computer running Windows Server 2003, and log on as **administrator@*domain*.contoso.com** (where *domain* is the name of your domain).

2. Click Start, and then click Network Connections to open the Network Connections window.

3. In the Network Connections window, right-click the Litware Inc Network connection, and then click Properties.

4. On the Litware Inc Network Connection Properties page, click Internet Protocol (TCP/IP), and then click Properties.

5. On the Internet Protocol (TCP/IP) Properties, in the Default Gateway box, type the IP address of your partner's Litware Inc Network connection, and then click OK.

6. On the Litware Inc Network Properties page, click Close to accept your changes.

Configuring IIS

IMPORTANT   *Complete this task from the student computer with the lower number. This will allow you to configure IIS on your server that runs Windows Server 2003.*

1. Start your computer running Windows Server 2003, and log on as **administrator@*domain*.contoso.com** (where *domain* is the name of your domain).

2. Click Start, select Administrative Tools, and then select Internet Information Services (IIS) Manager.

3. In the Internet Information Services (IIS) Manager console tree, expand Computer*xx* (where Computer*xx* is the name of your computer), and then expand Web Sites.

4. In the Internet Information Services (IIS) Manager console tree, right-click the Default Web Site, and then click Properties.

5. In the Web Site tab, in the IP Address drop-down list, click the IP address of the Contoso Ltd Network adapter that has been assigned to your student computer (10.1.1.*xx*), and then click OK.

6. Close the Internet Information Services (IIS) Manager console.

Verifying NAT Client Connectivity

> **IMPORTANT** *Complete this task from the student computer with the higher number. This will allow you to verify that the NAT client can communicate with a Web site on a different IP subnet.*

1. Start your computer running Windows Server 2003, and log on as **administrator@*domain*.contoso.com** (where *domain* is the name of your domain).

2. Click Start, point to All Programs, and then click Internet Explorer to open the Microsoft Internet Explorer window.

   If the Internet Explorer Enhanced Security Configure dialog box appears, click OK.

3. In the Internet Explorer Address bar, type **http://10.1.1.*xx*** (where 10.1.1.*xx* is the IP address of your partner's Contoso Ltd Network adapter), and then press ENTER.

   > **QUESTION** *Were you given the default page for the WWW service running on your partner's computer? Why or why not?*

4. Close Internet Explorer.

Removing NAT

> **IMPORTANT** *Complete this task from the student computer with the lower number. This will allow you to remove NAT from the student computer.*

1. Start your computer running Windows Server 2003, and log on as **student*xx*@*domain*.contoso.com** (where student*xx* is your student User Name and *domain* is the name of your domain).

2. Click Start, select Control Panel, and then double-click Administrative Tools.

3. Right-click Routing And Remote Access, and then select Run As to open the Run As dialog box.

4. In the Run As dialog box, select The Following User option, and then enter the following credentials in the dialog box fields to open the Routing And Remote Access console:

   a. In the User Name box, enter **administrator@*domain*.contoso.com** (where *domain* is the name of your domain).

   b. In the Password box, enter **MSPress@LS#1**.

5. Click OK to open the Routing And Remote Access console.

6. In the Routing And Remote Access console tree, expand Computer*xx* (where Computer*xx* is the name of your computer), and then expand IP Routing.

7. In the Routing And Remote Access console tree, right-click NAT/Basic Firewall, and then click Delete.

8. In the Routing And Remote Access dialog box, click Yes to remove NAT/Basic Firewall.

9. Close the Routing And Remote Access console.

Reconfiguring IIS

IMPORTANT   *Complete this task from the student computer with the lower number. This will allow you to configure IIS on your server that runs Windows Server 2003.*

1. Start your computer running Windows Server 2003, and log on as **administrator@*domain*.contoso.com** (where *domain* is the name of your domain).

2. Click Start, select Administrative Tools, and then select Internet Information Services (IIS) Manager.

3. In the Internet Information Services (IIS) Manager console tree, expand Computer*xx* (where Computer*xx* is the name of your computer), and then expand Web Sites.

4. In the Internet Information Services (IIS) Manager console tree, right-click the Default Web Site, and then click Properties.

5. In the Web Site tab, in the IP Address drop-down list, click All Unassigned, and then click OK.

6. Close the Internet Information Services (IIS) Manager console.

IMPORTANT   *You must reconnect the network cable to the Contoso Ltd Network adapter on the NAT client to complete future exercises.*

EXERCISE 8-6: CONFIGURING PACKET FILTERS

Estimated completion time: 10 minutes

You are testing Routing and Remote Access packet filters to determine how to block traffic to certain Transmission Control Protocol (TCP) ports that run on Windows Server 2003 servers on the network. To test this, you install IIS and now want to use the Routing and Remote Access packet filters to block Hypertext Transfer Protocol (HTTP) traffic to port 80.

Verifying IIS Client Connectivity

IMPORTANT *Complete this task from the student computer with the higher number. This will allow you to verify that the client computer can communicate with the Web server.*

1. Start your computer running Windows Server 2003, and log on as **administrator@*domain*.contoso.com** (where *domain* is the name of your domain).

2. Click Start, point to All Programs, and then click Internet Explorer to open the Internet Explorer window.

3. In the Internet Explorer Address bar, type **http://10.1.1.*xx*** (where 10.1.1.*xx* is the IP address of your partner's Contoso Ltd Network connection), and then press ENTER.

QUESTION *Were you given the default page for the WWW service running on your partner's computer?*

4. Close Internet Explorer.

IMPORTANT *If the Internet Explorer Enhanced Security Configure dialog box appears, click OK.*

Configuring a Packet Filter for HTTP Traffic

IMPORTANT *Complete this task from both student computers. This will allow you to create a Routing and Remote Access packet filter that will block HTTP traffic.*

1. Start your computer running Windows Server 2003, and log on as **student*xx*@*domain*.contoso.com** (where student*xx* is your student User Name and *domain* is the name of your domain).

2. Click Start, select Control Panel, and then double-click Administrative Tools.

3. Right-click Routing And Remote Access, and then select Run As to open the Run As dialog box.

4. In the Run As dialog box, select The Following User option, and then enter the following credentials in the dialog box fields to open the Routing And Remote Access console:

    a. In the User Name box, enter **administrator@*domain*.contoso.com** (where *domain* is the name of your domain).

    b. In the Password box, enter **MSPress@LS#1**.

5. Click OK to open the Routing And Remote Access console.

6. In the Routing And Remote Access console tree, expand Computer.*xx* (where Computer.*xx* is the name of your computer), and then expand IP Routing.

7. In the Routing And Remote Access console, click General, in the Details pane, right-click Contoso Ltd Network, and then select Properties.

8. In the General tab of the Contoso Ltd Network Properties page, click Inbound Filters to open the Inbound Filters page.

9. In the Inbound Filters dialog box, click New to open the Add IP Filter page.

10. On the Add IP Filter page, select the Destination Network check box, type **10.1.0.0** in the IP Address field, and then type **255.255.0.0** in the Subnet Mask field.

11. In the Protocol drop-down list, select TCP.

12. In the Destination port box, type **80**, and then click OK.

13. In the Inbound Filters page, verify that the Receive All Packets Except Those That Meet The Criteria Below option is selected, and then click OK.

14. On the Contoso Ltd Properties page, click OK.

15. Close the Routing And Remote Access console.

Testing the Packet Filter for HTTP Traffic

IMPORTANT   Complete this task from both student computers. This will allow you to test the HTTP packet filter that you created.

1. Start your computer running Windows Server 2003, and log on as **administrator@*domain*.contoso.com** (where *domain* is the name of your domain).

2. Click Start, point to All Programs, and then click Internet Explorer to open the Internet Explorer window.

   If the Internet Explorer Enhanced Security Configure dialog box appears, click OK.

3. In the Internet Explorer Address bar, type **http://10.1.1.*xx*** (where 10.1.1.*xx* is the IP address of your partner's Contoso Ltd connection), and then press ENTER.

   QUESTION   Were you given the default page for the WWW service running on your partner's computer? Why or why not?

4. Close Internet Explorer.

EXERCISE 8-7: REMOVING ROUTING AND REMOTE ACCESS

Estimated completion time: 10 minutes

In this exercise, you will remove Routing and Remote Access configurations that were created and configured in the previous exercises. Doing so will remove any dependencies that can influence later exercises.

Removing Routing and Remote Access

> **IMPORTANT**   Complete this task from both student computers. This will allow you to remove any Routing and Remote Access configurations that were made during Lab 8.

1. Start your computer running Windows Server 2003, and log on as **administrator@*domain*.contoso.com** (where *domain* is the name of your domain).

2. Click Start, select Control Panel, double-click Administrative Tools, and then double-click Routing And Remote Access.

3. In the Routing And Remote Access console tree, right-click Computer*xx* (where Computer*xx* is the name of your computer), and then click Disable Routing And Remote Access.

4. In the Routing And Remote Access dialog box, click Yes to continue.

5. Close all open windows.

LAB REVIEW QUESTIONS

Estimated completion time: 15 minutes

1. What two VPN protocols can be used with Windows Server 2003?

2. What two types of routes can be added to a routing table?

3. What is one method that you could use to configure a packet filter to block Telnet traffic using the Routing and Remote Access service?

4. Which two types of interfaces are added to a NAT configuration?

5. Which three dial-in settings are configured on a specific user's account properties?

6. What are two components of a remote access policy?

7. What would happen if the two network interfaces used in NAT were reversed?

LAB CHALLENGE 8-1: DESIGNING A REMOTE ACCESS SOLUTION

Estimated completion time: 20 minutes

You are the network administrator for Trey Research, which is located in Denver. Trey Research recently added two new branch office locations to expand its operations. The first branch office is a manufacturing and research facility located in Dallas. The users on the network in Dallas must be able to transmit confidential information to the main office in Denver. The second branch office, a facility for the Administrative and Finance departments, is located in Kansas City. The users on the network in Kansas City must be able to transmit financial information to the main office in Denver. These users also will use portable computers when they travel to the main office. You must control the length of time they are allowed to connect when they connect to the Routing and Remote Access server onsite in Denver using their wireless network adapters. Each branch office has two servers onsite that run Windows Server 2003. Each new branch office location will be connected using a 256-Kbps digital subscriber line (DSL) connection that is connected through an Internet service provider (ISP). Each of these must be secured using the highest encryption available. The current IP addressing for Trey Research is as follows:

- Main office: 172.16.0.0/24

- Dallas: 10.10.10.0/24

- Kansas City: 172.16.0.0/16

Trey Research also recently purchased a distribution center located in Atlanta. The company does not want to incur unnecessary expenses when connecting the distribution center to the main office. All orders will be faxed to the distribution center. The users in Atlanta then must be able to access order status and order-processing information using IIS 6 on a computer located at the main office that runs Windows Server 2003. The Atlanta branch office is connected to the Denver office by a dedicated 56-Kbps frame relay connection. The network in Atlanta currently uses the 192.168.0.0/24 network address. There are two servers that run Windows Server 2003 onsite in Atlanta. How can you use the material covered in this lab to configure a network to meet all of these needs?

LAB 9
MAINTAINING A NETWORK INFRASTRUCTURE

This lab contains the following exercises and activities:

- Exercise 9-1: Using Task Manager
- Exercise 9-2: Using the Performance Console
- Exercise 9-3: Monitoring Network Traffic
- Exercise 9-4: Troubleshooting Connectivity
- Exercise 9-5: Configuring Windows Server 2003 Services
- Exercise 9-6: Removing Installed Components
- Lab Review Questions
- Lab Challenge 9-1: Monitoring and Troubleshooting a Network

After completing this lab, you will be able to:

- Use Task Manager to view real-time statistics.
- Add and remove performance counters.
- Configure performance alerts.
- Monitor network traffic using Network Monitor.
- Use various troubleshooting tools.
- Configure Microsoft Windows Server 2003 services.

Estimated completion time: 115 minutes (This estimate includes the Before You Begin setup procedures.)

BEFORE YOU BEGIN

Estimated completion time: 10 minutes

> **IMPORTANT** If you have not completed the exercises in Lab 4, "Managing and Monitoring DNS," you must complete the following prerequisite procedures.

Installing Windows Server 2003 Support Tools

IMPORTANT *Complete this task from both student computers. This will allow you to install the Microsoft Windows Server 2003 Support Tools on your student computer.*

1. Start your computer running Windows Server 2003, and log on as **administrator@*domain*.contoso.com** (where *domain* is the name of your domain).

2. Click Start, and then click My Computer.

3. In the My Computer window, right-click the drive that represents your CD-ROM drive, and then click Open. (Your Microsoft Windows Server 2003 installation CD-ROM should be in the CD-ROM drive.)

4. Open the Support folder, open the Tools folder, and then double-click Suptools.msi.

5. In the Windows Support Tools Setup Wizard window, click Next.

6. On the End User License Agreement page, review the license agreement and then click I Agree if you agree with the terms. (If you do not agree with the terms, you cannot continue with this installation.) Click Next.

7. On the User Information page, accept the default name and organization, and then click Next to continue.

8. On the Destination Directory page, click Install Now to begin the installation.

9. On the Completing The Windows Support Tools Setup Wizard page, click Finish to complete the installation of the Windows Support Tools.

10. Close all open windows.

Installing the WWW and FTP Services

IMPORTANT *Complete this task from both student computers. This will allow you to install the World Wide Web (WWW) service and the File Transfer Protocol (FTP) service on your server computer that runs Windows Server 2003.*

1. Start your computer running Windows Server 2003, and log on as **administrator@*domain*.contoso.com** (where *domain* is the name of your domain).

2. Click Start, select Control Panel, and then click Add Or Remove Programs.

3. In the Add Or Remove Programs window, click Add/Remove Windows Components.

4. In the Windows Components Wizard, in the Components section, select the Application Server option, and then click the Details button.

5. In the Application Server window, select Internet Information Services (IIS), and then click the Details button.

6. In the Internet Information Services (IIS) window, select File Transfer Protocol (FTP) Service and World Wide Web Service, and then click OK.

7. In the Internet Information Services (IIS) window, click OK.

8. In the Application Server window, click OK.

9. In the Windows Components Wizard, click Next.

10. If asked for the location of the installation files, place the Windows Server 2003 installation CD into the CD-ROM drive, and then click OK.

11. On the Completing The Windows Components Wizard page, click Finish.

12. Close all open windows.

Configuring the WWW and FTP Services

> **IMPORTANT** *Complete this task from both student computers. This will allow you to configure the WWW and FTP services on your server computer that runs Windows Server 2003.*

1. Start your computer running Windows Server 2003, and log on as **administrator@*domain*.contoso.com** (where *domain* is the name of your domain).

2. Click Start, point to All Programs, select Accessories, and then click Notepad to open Microsoft Notepad.

3. In the Untitled—Notepad window, type the following text:

```
<html>
<head>
<title>Welcome to the World Wide Web</title>
</head>
<body>
<p><font color="#0066CC"
face="Arial"><b>This is the default page for the World
Wide Web service!!</b></font></p>
</body>
</html>
```

4. In the Untitled—Notepad window, click File, and then click Save As.

5. In the Save As window, click the My Computer icon on the left, and then navigate to the C:\Inetpub\Wwwroot folder.

6. In the Save As window, in the File Name box, type **default.htm**, and then click Save to save the Default.htm file to the C:\Inetpub\Wwwroot folder.

   If prompted to overwrite an existing Default.htm file, click Yes to proceed.

7. Close all open windows.

SCENARIO

You are the network administrator for Contoso, Ltd. In recent months, you have deployed several server computers that run Windows Server 2003 on your network. Each of the servers operates different network services. You have received various reports from users that some of the servers might be experiencing problems. Windows Server 2003 and the Support Tools include several utilities that can be used to gather statistics and troubleshoot connectivity problems, and with them you have decided to monitor server usage and troubleshoot network connectivity.

EXERCISE 9-1: USING TASK MANAGER

Estimated completion time: 10 minutes

Since your users have been reporting that they are having network problems, you first must gather real-time server statistics on your servers.

Viewing Processes

IMPORTANT   Complete this task from both student computers. This will allow you to view the process that your Windows Server 2003 computer is currently running.

1. Start your computer running Windows Server 2003, and log on as **administrator@*domain*.contoso.com** (where *domain* is the name of your domain).

2. Press CTRL+ALT+DEL to open the Windows Security window.

3. In the Windows Security window, click Task Manager to open the Windows Task Manager window. Leave Task Manager open.

4. Click Start, click Run, type **notepad** in the Open box, and then press ENTER.

5. Click Start, click Run, type **wordpad** in the Open box, and then press ENTER.

QUESTION   Are the Microsoft Notepad and Microsoft WordPad applications listed in the Applications tab in Windows Task Manager?

6. In the Windows Task Manager window, click the Processes tab.

QUESTION   Are the Notepad.exe and WordPad.exe processes listed in the Processes tab in Windows Task Manager?

7. In the Processes tab, in the Image Name column, click Notepad.exe, and then click End Process.

8. In the Task Manager Warning dialog box, click Yes to confirm the termination of the process. Notice that the Notepad window closes.

9. In the Processes tab, in the Image Name column, click Wordpad.exe, and then click End Process.

10. In the Task Manager Warning dialog box, click Yes to confirm the termination of the process. Notice that the WordPad window closes.

11. Close the Windows Task Manager window.

Viewing Real-Time Performance Data

IMPORTANT   Complete this task from both student computers. This will allow you to view real-time central processing unit (CPU) usage on your computer.

1. Start your computer running Windows Server 2003, and log on as **administrator@*domain*.contoso.com** (where *domain* is the name of your domain).

2. Press CTRL+ALT+DEL to open the Windows Security window.

3. In the Windows Security window, click Task Manager to open Windows Task Manager. Leave Task Manager open.

4. In the Windows Task Manager window, click the Performance tab.

5. Click Start, click Run, type **calc** in the Open box, and then press ENTER to open Microsoft Calculator.

6. In the Calculator window, click View, and then click Scientific.

7. On the numeric keypad in Calculator, click 999 and then click x^3 several times to generate CPU and page file statistics. Notice that the CPU usage increases as displayed in Task Manager.

8. Close all open windows.

Viewing Real-Time Networking Data

NOTE   Complete this task from both student computers. This will allow you to view networking usage on your server computer that runs Windows Server 2003.

1. Start your computer running Windows Server 2003, and log on as **administrator@*domain*.contoso.com** (where *domain* is the name of your domain).

2. Press CTRL+ALT+DEL to open the Windows Security window.

3. In the Windows Security window, click Task Manager to open Windows Task Manager. Leave Task Manager open.

4. In the Windows Task Manager window, click the Networking tab.

5. Click Start, click Run, and then type **computer*xx*\c$** (where computer*xx* is the name of your partner's computer) in the Open box.

6. In the Computer*xx* window (where Computer*xx* is the name of your partner's computer), right-click the Program Files folder, and then click Copy.

7. Right-click an empty space on the desktop of your server, and then click Paste.

   As the files are copied to your server computer, notice that utilization of the local area network (LAN) adapter increases.

8. Delete the Program Files folder from your desktop.

9. Close all open windows.

EXERCISE 9-2: USING THE PERFORMANCE CONSOLE

Estimated completion time: 15 minutes

The next step in gathering information about the performance of your computers running Windows Server 2003 is to troubleshoot your server problems by using the Performance console with specific counters.

Adding and Removing Counters

IMPORTANT   *Complete this task from both student computers. This will allow you to add and remove performance counters.*

1. Start your computer running Windows Server 2003, and log on as **administrator@*domain*.contoso.com** (where *domain* is the name of your domain).

2. Click Start, select Administrative Tools, and then select Performance to start the Performance console.

3. In the Performance console, delete the counters in the default System Monitor view. (Hint: Click the X on the icon menu bar.)

4. In the scope pane, select System Monitor under Console Root.

5. In the Performance console, in the details pane, click the plus (+) icon to add Performance Monitor counters.

6. In the Add Counters dialog box, in the Performance Object drop-down list, click Processor. In the Select Counters From List section, click %Processor Time, and then click Add.

7. In the Add Counters dialog box, in the Performance Object drop-down list, click Memory. In the Select Counters From List section, click Available Bytes, and then click Add.

8. In the Add Counters dialog box, in the Performance Object drop-down list, click PhysicalDisk. In the Select Counters From List section, click %Disk Read Time, and then click Add.

9. In the Add Counters dialog box, in the Performance Object drop-down list, click Network Interface. In the Select Counters From List section, click Bytes Total/Sec, and then click Add.

10. Click Close to close the Add Counters dialog box, and then minimize the Performance console.

Viewing Performance Statistics

IMPORTANT   *Complete this task from both student computers. This will allow you to add and remove performance counters.*

1. Start your computer running Windows Server 2003, and log on as **administrator@*domain*.contoso.com** (where *domain* is the name of your domain).

2. Click Start, select Administrative Tools, and then select Computer Management.

3. In the Computer Management console, in the console tree under Storage, click Disk Defragmenter.

4. In the details pane, click Analyze.

5. When disk defragmentation analysis is complete, click Close to close the Analysis Complete message.

6. Close Computer Management, and then maximize Performance.

7. In the details pane, click the Freeze Display button (the red circle with a white X) or press CTRL+F.

8. At the bottom of the details pane, under Counter, verify that %Processor Time is selected.

9. Hold down the CTRL key, and then press H to highlight the currently selected counter.

10. Use the up and down arrow keys on your keyboard to view the other counters.

QUESTION   *Which system resources did Disk Defragmenter use?*

Creating and Configuring an Alert

IMPORTANT   *Complete this task from both student computers. This will allow you to configure an alert message that will be sent to the administrator.*

1. Start your computer running Windows Server 2003, and log on as **administrator@*domain*.contoso.com** (where *domain* is the name of your domain).

2. Click Start, select Administrative Tools, and select Performance to start the Performance console.

3. In the Performance console, expand Performance Logs And Alerts, and then right-click Alerts.

4. On the shortcut menu, select New Alert Settings.

5. In the New Alert Settings dialog box, type **disk time,** and then click OK.

6. In the Disk Time page, in the General tab, click Add.

7. In the Add Counters page, in the Performance object drop-down list, select PhysicalDisk.

8. In the Select Counters From list, select %Disk Time, and then click Add.

9. Click Close to close to the Add Counters page.

10. On the Disk Time page, in the General tab, in the Limit box, type **50**.

11. On the Disk Time page, in the General tab, in the Interval box, type **5**.

12. In the Run As box, verify that <Default> is selected.

13. In the Action tab, select Send A Network Message To, and then type **administrator**.

14. In the Schedule tab, under Start Scan, verify that Manually is selected, and then click OK.

15. In the Performance console select Alerts, and in the details pane, right-click the Disk Time alert, and then select Start.

    The Disk Time alert turns green, indicating that the alert was started.

16. Close the Performance console.

Configuring the Messenger Service to Start

IMPORTANT   Complete this task from both student computers. This will allow you to receive notification of the alert you configured in the preceding exercise: "Creating and Configuring an Alert."

1. Start your computer running Windows Server 2003, and log on as **administrator@*domain*.contoso.com** (where *domain* is the name of your domain).

2. Click Start, click Control Panel, double-click Administrative Tools, and then double-click Services.

3. In the Services console details pane, locate and then double-click the Messenger service in the list of local services.

4. On the Messenger Properties (Local Computer) page, in the General tab, in the Startup Type list, select Manual, and then click Apply.

5. Click Start to start the Messenger service on the local computer.

6. Click OK to close the Messenger Properties (Local Computer) page.

7. Close the Services console.

Triggering an Alert

IMPORTANT *Complete this task from both student computers. This will allow you to trigger the alert and receive notification.*

1. Start your computer running Windows Server 2003, and log on as **administrator@*domain*.contoso.com** (where *domain* is the name of your domain).

2. Click Start, and then click My Computer to open the My Computer window.

3. In the My Computer window, right-click the C drive, and then click Properties.

4. In the Local Disk (C:) Properties page, click the Tools tab.

5. In the Tools tab, in the Defragmentation section, click Defragment Now to open the Disk Defragmenter window.

6. In the Disk Defragmenter window, click Defragment.

   To see the alert, wait before closing all open windows.

7. After you receive the alert, close all open windows.

Stopping the Alert

IMPORTANT *Complete this task from both student computers. This will allow you to stop the alert you created in the preceding steps.*

1. Start your computer running Windows Server 2003, and log on as **administrator@*domain*.contoso.com** (where *domain* is the name of your domain).

2. Click Start, click Control Panel, and then double-click Administrative Tools.

3. Double-click Performance to start the Performance console.

4. In the Performance console, expand Performance Logs And Alerts, and then click Alerts.

5. In the details pane, select the Disk Time alert, right-click the Disk Time alert, and then click Stop.

EXERCISE 9-3: MONITORING NETWORK TRAFFIC

Estimated completion time: 15 minutes

After gathering local computer information and statistics to troubleshoot network connectivity issues, you must now gather information about the network traffic.

Installing Network Monitor

IMPORTANT   *Complete this task from both student computers. This will allow you to install Network Monitor on your server computer that runs Windows Server 2003. Network Monitor will then be used to inspect network packets received by the server.*

1. Start your computer running Windows Server 2003, and log on as **administrator@*domain*.contoso.com** (where *domain* is the name of your domain).

2. Click Start, select Control Panel, and then click Add Or Remove Programs.

3. In the Add Or Remove Programs window, click Add/Remove Windows Components.

4. In the Windows Components Wizard, in the Components section, select the Management And Monitoring Tools option, and then click the Details button.

5. In the Management And Monitoring Tools window, check the Network Monitor Tools check box, and then click OK.

6. Click Next in the Windows Components Wizard.

7. If asked for the location of the installation files, place the Windows Server 2003 installation CD into the CD-ROM drive, and then click OK.

8. Click Finish on the Completing The Windows Components Wizard page.

9. Close all open windows.

Capturing and Filtering FTP Data Using Network Monitor

IMPORTANT   *Complete this task from both student computers. This will allow you to open a session with the FTP service on your partner's computer.*

1. Start your computer running Windows Server 2003, and log on as **administrator@*domain*.contoso.com** (where *domain* is the name of your domain).

2. Click Start, click Control Panel, click Administrative Tools, and then click Network Monitor.

3. If prompted for the network adapter, click the Contoso Ltd Network adapter, and then click OK.

4. In the Microsoft Network Monitor window, click Capture on the toolbar, and then click Start.

IMPORTANT   *Wait for your partner to complete the preceding steps before you proceed.*

5. Click Start, point to All Programs, and then click Internet Explorer to open Microsoft Internet Explorer.

6. In the Internet Explorer dialog box, select the In The Future, Do Not Show This Message option, and then click OK.

7. In the Internet Explorer Address bar, type **ftp://computer.xx** (where computer.xx is the name of your partner's computer).

   IMPORTANT   Wait for your partner to complete the preceding steps before stopping the capture.

8. In the Microsoft Network Monitor window, click Capture on the toolbar, and then click Stop And View.

9. In the Microsoft Network Monitor window, Capture: 1 (Summary) window, click Display on the toolbar, and then click Filter.

10. In the Display Filter window, click the Protocol = = Any option, and then click Edit Expression.

11. In the Expression window, in the Protocol tab, click the Disable All button.

12. In the Disabled Protocols section, select FTP, click the Enable button, and then click OK.

    Take a minute to observe what kind of data Network Monitor has collected.

13. In the Display Filter window, click OK.

14. Close the Network Monitor window.

15. When you are prompted to save the capture in the Microsoft Network Monitor dialog box, click No.

16. Close all open windows.

Capturing and Filtering HTTP Data Using Network Monitor

   IMPORTANT   Complete this task from both student computers. This will allow you to open a session with the Hypertext Transfer Protocol (HTTP) service on your partner's computer.

1. Start your computer running Windows Server 2003, and log on as **administrator@domain.contoso.com** (where domain is the name of your domain).

2. Click Start, click Control Panel, click Administrative Tools, and then click Network Monitor.

3. If prompted for the network, click the Contoso Ltd Network, and then click OK.

4. In the Microsoft Network Monitor window, click Capture on the toolbar, and then click Start.

   IMPORTANT   Wait until your partner has completed the preceding steps before you proceed.

5. Click Start, point to All Programs, and then click Internet Explorer.

6. In the Internet Explorer dialog box, select the In The Future, Do Not Show This Message option, and then click OK.

7. In the Internet Explorer Address bar, type **http://computer*xx*** (where computer*xx* is the name of your partner's computer).

   IMPORTANT   Wait for your partner to complete the preceding steps before stopping the capture.

8. In the Microsoft Network Monitor window, click Capture on the toolbar, and then click Stop And View.

9. In the Microsoft Network Monitor window, Capture: 1 (Summary) window, click Display on the toolbar, and then click Filter.

10. In the Display Filter window, click the Protocol = = Any option, and then click Edit Expression.

11. In the Expression window, in the Protocol tab, click the Disable All button.

12. In the Disabled Protocols section, select HTTP, click the Enable button, and then click OK.

13. In the Display Filter window, click OK.

   Take a minute to observe the data Network Monitor collected.

14. Close the Network Monitor window.

15. When you are prompted to save the capture in the Microsoft Network Monitor dialog box, click No.

16. Close all open windows.

EXERCISE 9-4: TROUBLESHOOTING CONNECTIVITY

Estimated completion time: 15 minutes

Users on the Contoso network report having problems connecting to the server and connecting to other resources such as the Internet. In this exercise, you will use several Windows Server 2003 utilities to troubleshoot connectivity problems.

Using Ipconfig

IMPORTANT   Complete this task from both student computers. This will allow you to verify the Internet Protocol (IP) addressing configuration on your server computers that run Windows Server 2003.

1. Start your computer running Windows Server 2003, and log on as **administrator@*domain*.contoso.com** (where *domain* is the name of your domain).

2. Click Start, click Run, type **cmd** in the Open box, and then press ENTER.

3. In the command prompt window, at the command prompt, type
ipconfig /?, and then press ENTER.

QUESTION   Which switches are available when using the Ipconfig utility?

4. In the command prompt window, at the command prompt, type
ipconfig /all. Record the information the command provides for the
Contoso Ltd Network adapter in the space below:

IP address:_____

Subnet mask:_____

Default gateway:_____

DNS servers:_____

Host name:_____

Physical address: _____

5. Close all open windows.

Using Tracert

IMPORTANT   Complete this task from both student computers. This will allow
you to use the Tracert utility to verify connectivity to another Transmission Control Protocol/Internet Protocol (TCP/IP) host.

1. Start your computer running Windows Server 2003, and log on as
administrator@*domain*.contoso.com (where *domain* is the name of
your domain).

2. Click Start, click Run, type **cmd** in the Open box, and then press ENTER.

3. In the command prompt window, at the command prompt, type
tracert instructor01.contoso.com, and then press ENTER.

QUESTION   How many hops did it take to reach the destination?

QUESTION   What is the IP address of the host instructor.contoso.com?

4. Close all open windows.

Using PathPing

> **IMPORTANT**   Complete this task from both student computers. This will allow you to use the PathPing utility to verify connectivity to another TCP/IP host.

1. Start your computer running Windows Server 2003, and log on as **administrator@*domain*.contoso.com** (where *domain* is the name of your domain).

2. Click Start, click Run, type **cmd** in the Open box, and then press ENTER.

3. In the command prompt window, at the command prompt, type **pathping instructor01.contoso.com**, and then press ENTER.

> **QUESTION**   What is the percentage of packets that were lost?

4. Close all open windows.

Using Netstat

> **IMPORTANT**   Complete this task from both student computers. This will allow you to use the Netstat utility to display protocol and TCP and User Datagram Protocol (UDP) port information on your server computer that runs Windows Server 2003.

1. Start your computer running Windows Server 2003, and log on as **administrator@*domain*.contoso.com** (where *domain* is the name of your domain).

2. Click Start, click Run, type **cmd** in the Open box, and then press ENTER.

3. In the command prompt window, at the command prompt, type **netstat -na**, and then press ENTER.

> **QUESTION**   Which TCP/UDP ports are being used on your computer?

4. Close all open windows.

Using Netdiag

> **IMPORTANT**   Complete this task from both student computers. This will allow you to use the Netdiag utility to help you troubleshoot networking connectivity.

1. Start your computer running Windows Server 2003, and log on as **administrator@*domain*.contoso.com** (where *domain* is the name of your domain).

2. Click Start, point to All Programs, click Windows Support Tools, and then click Command Prompt.

3. In the command prompt window, at the C:\Program Files\Support Tools prompt, type **netdiag /l**, and then press ENTER.

4. Click Start, click My Computer, and then browse for and double-click the C:\Documents and Settings\Administrator folder.

5. In the C:\Program Files\Support Tools window, locate and double-click the Netdiag.log.

> **QUESTION**   What types of information does the Netdiag utility show? (Hint: Use the log file to record your answers.)

EXERCISE 9-5: CONFIGURING WINDOWS SERVER 2003 SERVICES

Estimated completion time: 15 minutes

You made several configuration changes in the previous exercises while trouble-shooting, and some will require you to stop and start Windows Server 2003 services. After completing the installation and configuration steps, you now must view and configure Windows Server 2003 services on your servers.

Viewing Service Dependencies

> **IMPORTANT**   Complete this task from both student computers. This will allow you to view Windows Server 2003 service dependencies.

1. Start your computer running Windows Server 2003, and log on as **administrator@*domain*.contoso.com** (where *domain* is the name of your domain).

2. Click Start, click Control Panel, and then double-click Administrative Tools.

3. In the Administrative Tools window, double-click Services.

4. In the Services console details pane, double-click World Wide Web Publishing Service.

5. On the World Wide Web Publishing Service (Local Computer) page, click the Dependencies tab.

> **QUESTION**   Which other services does the World Wide Web Publishing Service depend on? (Hint: Look in the This Service Depends On The Following System Components section.)

> **QUESTION**   Which services depend on the World Wide Web Publishing Service? (Hint: Look in the The Following System Components Depend On This Service section.)

6. In the World Wide Web Publishing Service (Local Computer) page, click OK.

Configuring Service Startup Options

IMPORTANT   *Complete this task from both student computers. This will allow you to configure the Startup Options for a Windows Server 2003 service.*

1. Start your computer running Windows Server 2003, and log on as **administrator@*domain*.contoso.com** (where *domain* is the name of your domain).

2. Click Start, click Control Panel, and then double-click Administrative Tools.

3. In the Administrative Tools window, double-click Services.

4. In the Services console details pane, double-click the Telnet service.

QUESTION   *What is the Service Status of the Telnet service on your computer?*

5. Click OK to close the Telnet Properties page.

6. Leave the Services console open.

7. Click Start, click Run, type **cmd** in the Open box, and then press ENTER.

8. In the command prompt window, type **telnet computer*xx*** (where computer*xx* is the name of your computer), and then press ENTER.

QUESTION   *What error is reported when you try to connect using Telnet?*

9. Close the command prompt window.

10. In the Services console, double-click the Telnet service.

11. On the Telnet Properties (Local Computer) page, in the Startup Type drop-down list, select Automatic, and then click OK to close the Telnet Properties page.

12. Close all open windows, and then restart your server computer.

13. Start your computer running Windows Server 2003, and log on as **administrator@*domain*.contoso.com** (where *domain* is the name of your domain).

14. Click Start, click Control Panel, and then double-click Administrative Tools.

15. In the Administrative Tools window, double-click Services.

16. In the Services console details pane, double-click the Telnet service.

QUESTION   *What is the Service Status of the Telnet service on your computer?*

17. Click Start, click Run, type **cmd** in the Open box, and then press ENTER.

18. In the command prompt window, type **telnet computer*xx*** (where computer*xx* is the name of your computer), and then press ENTER.

    If you are prompted for credentials, provide the following:

    a. Login: **administrator**

    b. Password: **MSPress@LS#1**

    QUESTION Can you connect to the Telnet service running on your student computer?

19. Close all open windows.

Starting and Stopping Services

> **IMPORTANT** Complete this task from both student computers. This will allow you to start and stop a Windows Server 2003 service on your computer.

1. Start your computer running Windows Server 2003, and log on as **administrator@*domain*.contoso.com** (where *domain* is the name of your domain).

2. Click Start, click Control Panel, and then double-click Administrative Tools.

3. In the Administrative Tools window, double-click Services.

4. In the Services console details pane, double-click the Telnet service.

5. On the Telnet Properties page, in the Service Status section, click Stop to stop the Telnet service.

6. On the Telnet Properties page, in the Service Status section, click Start to start the Telnet service.

7. Close all open windows.

EXERCISE 9-6: REMOVING INSTALLED COMPONENTS

Estimated completion time: 5 minutes

In this exercise you will remove the configuration settings that were created or configured in the previous exercises. Doing so removes any dependencies that can influence subsequent lab exercises.

Removing Internet Information Services (IIS)

> **IMPORTANT** Complete this task from both student computers. This will allow you to remove Internet Information Services (IIS) from your server computer that runs Windows Server 2003.

1. Start your computer running Windows Server 2003, and log on as **administrator@*domain*.contoso.com** (where *domain* is the name of your domain).

2. Click Start, click Control Panel, and then click Add Or Remove Programs.

3. In the Add Or Remove Programs window, click Add/Remove Windows Components.

4. In the Windows Components Wizard, in the Components section, select the Application Server option, and then click the Details button.

5. In the Application Server window, clear the Internet Information Services (IIS) check box, and then click OK.

6. In the Windows Components Wizard, click Next.

7. On the Completing The Windows Components Wizard page, click Finish.

8. Close all open windows.

LAB REVIEW QUESTIONS

Estimated completion time: 15 minutes

1. Name five utilities that can be used on a computer running Windows Server 2003 to assist in troubleshooting a networking problem.

2. Which types of packets can Network Monitor be used to capture?

3. What are the three startup options available for a Windows Server 2003 service?

4. What are the four tabs in Task Manager that can be used for troubleshooting?

5. Which Windows Server 2003 utilities can be used to verify connectivity to another TCP/IP host?

6. Which Windows Server 2003 utilities can be used to view IP statistics and configuration information about a server computer?

7. Which two utilities can be used to view real-time performance statistics on a server computer running Windows Server 2003?

LAB CHALLENGE 9-1: MONITORING AND TROUBLESHOOTING A NETWORK

Estimated completion time: 15 minutes

You are the network administrator for a child domain of contoso.com. You currently have two domain controllers for the child domain. As part of a network audit, you must document the configurations of your child domain network servers. This information should include the IP address, Media Access Control (MAC) address, open TCP/UDP ports, and DNS configuration on the servers. You have already implemented the Remote Desktop for Administration feature on your networked servers, but now you need the ability to Telnet from one domain controller to another to copy several documents. You must configure Telnet to not start until after the systems are rebooted because of the potential security risk. Create a plan to perform this audit and configure Telnet correctly.